Drinking at the Sources

An appeal to the Jew and the Christian to note
their common beginnings

Jacques Doukhan

Translated by Walter R. Beach
and Robert M. Johnston

Pacific Press Publishing Association
Mountain View, California
Oshawa, Ontario

In memory of my father
of his light
of his suffering

Library of Congress Cataloging in Publication Data

Doukhan, Jacques.
   Drinking at the sources.

   Translation of: Boire aux sources.
   1. Judaism—Relations—Christianity. 2. Christianity
and other religions—Judaism. I. Title.
BM535.D6313   261.2'6   81-634
ISBN 0-8163-0407-6   AACR2

"The day one gives an account of truth without betraying the sources, that day the Messiah will come." —TALMUD

"Whoever," replied Jesus, "drinks the water I will give him will never thirst. Indeed, the water which I will give him will become in him a spring of water welling up to eternal life." —THE GOSPEL

Note From the Publisher

Perusing the introductory pages, the reader will no doubt be surprised that the author has invited *two* writers to contribute prefatory remarks to his manuscript. One foreword is the general rule. Jacques Doukhan believes that his presentation will gain in understanding and acceptance if introduced by these two well-known men.

The author respects the personal perspective with which each reader—whether Jewish or Christian—approaches this book. But, he asks, why should the reader be given only one set of options—a single foreword? Would it not be better to offer the reader the viewpoints of both a Jew and a Christian? In this way the two streams would flow parallel from the beginning.

Why the author would solicit the help of André Chouraqui* and F. Lovsky† should be obvious. The first, particularly by his recent translation of the Gospels, has built a new bridge between Jews and Christians. The second, because of an abiding interest in the history of the unhappy relations between the church and the synagogue, likewise has endeavored to close the breach. These two very knowledgeable men are well qualified to express an opinion on Dr. Doukhan's book—one further effort to break down walls of animosity and contempt.

Drinking at the Sources deals with the Judeo-Christian drama, especially focusing on the sharp conflict between the two communities. Dr. Doukhan's goal is to bring about a reconciliation between them.

---

*President of the Union of Hebrew Culture. Vice mayor (1965-1969) and municipal councillor of Jerusalem. Director of the collection *Sinai* published by the Presses Universitaires of France. Author of numerous books, including *The State of Israel, History of Judaism, The Jews* (a dialog between Cardinal J. Daniélou and A. Chouraqui), and *Letter to an Arab Friend,* and *Letter to a Christian Friend.*

†Member of a working group called Church and People of Israel, sponsored by the Protestant Federation of France. Editor of *Jewish Studies,* sponsored by the Reformed Church review, *Faith and Life.* Author of *Anti-Semitism and the Mystery of Israel, Christian Anti-Semitism,* and *The Cleft of Absence.*

CONTENTS

Foreword

The reader will have no difficulty sensing the depth and the complexity of the drama that Jacques Doukhan analyzes in this volume. He thinks of his effort as an anguished cry born of despair—an impassioned search for the way out of a dilemma. But on what plane does he operate? Is it that of theology, or psychology? Or both?

The schism between Israel and the Church is rooted in the most profound realities of history; it cannot be understood unless one has constantly in mind the historical perspectives of that schism. The worst temptation that can befall one—here, as elsewhere—is to project into the past, conditions as they exist at present; that is, to proceed as if at the time of Jesus Christianity and Judaism existed as they do today or as they did following the conversion of Constantine in the fourth century.

Another error, just as palpable and consequential, is to consider the trial of Jesus divorced from context and thus make of it an academic debate solely between experts. But Philo had declared before the four Gospels were written that the high priest of the temple of Jerusalem was the Son of God and of Wisdom. Was *he* crucified for that?

When Jesus said that He was the Messiah, was His contention not to have consequences in a land occupied by Roman legions since 66 B.C.? In a land where leaders of resistance movements had regularly been proclaimed king and messiah of Israel by their troops? Alas, messianic adventures were not uncommon in those times! Many of them ended in atrocious massacres—from Judas the Galilean, who preached revolt against Rome when Jesus was a child, to Bar-Kokhba.

Because Israel lived constantly under the threat of extermination by pagan, barbarian, and imperial Rome, were not the men responsible for her well-being and destiny to be extremely concerned by the rising tide of

9

another messianic movement? And especially since this latest manifestation was led by a self-proclaimed christ with an overpowering personality? The word from Caiaphas that it was to their advantage that one man should die to save the nation must be understood in the light of the stark reality of Roman repression, which, according to Tacitus, was responsible for 600,000 crucified victims.

Furthermore, it is absurd to set Christianity against Judaism before the second century. Israel, at the time of Christ, was divided into a multitude of schools and sects, which opposed one another in bitter struggles. The ferocity of contention was fueled by each camp's desire to be the spiritual leader of the Jewish people.

Only two sects survived the Roman massacres of A.D. 70 and A.D. 134—the Pharisees and the Christians. The first was to lead the survivors of the Jewish-Roman war in saving the vestiges of the past while awaiting the salvation of Israel. The second was driven from the synagogues by the Pharisees, who eventually assumed monolithic control over Judaism.

The schism between these two groups underwent a change of character after the destruction of the Jerusalem temple in A.D. 70. Relations between Pharisaic Judaism and the Christians worsened significantly in A.D. 134 following the attempt at genocide perpetrated under Hadrian. But the schism widened to grievous dimensions following the conversion of Constantine in the fourth century, when Christianity was made the official religion of an empire which Judaism hated not only because (1) it was pagan, but still more because (2) the Roman Empire had put an end to the kingdom of Judea—the last terrestrial hope of Israel before the awaited hour of her "resurrection."

Rome had devastated Athens, destroyed the sources of Gallic culture, and almost succeeded in its attempted genocide against the Jews before it became officially Christian and the seat of papal authority. After the fourth century the Judeo-Christian conflict took on the characteristics denounced by Jacques Doukhan. But even then theological controversies masked the real reasons for the schism, which can be found only in the historical situations and aspirations of both the Church and Israel:

The Church set out to win the Greco-Latin world to the Christ-King. Israel, for all practical purposes, shut itself off from that world in an effort to preserve the language and culture of the Hebrew tradition, as set forth in the Hebrew Scriptures. Israel's hopes leaned forward to the hour of her redemption as a people and a place centering in Jerusalem.

* * *

This volume that Jacques Doukhan offers for our meditation produces

10

an eerie feeling. I finished reading it here in Jerusalem, the capital of the state of Israel and of a resurrected Hebrew culture.

The anti-Semitism which causes Jacques Doukhan's cruel suffering (and which has resulted in so many victims) does not exist here. Our Jewish children today find it difficult to understand what that disease meant to their forebears. In Israel, the Christians and the Muslims constitute the minorities. They suffer at times, not only because of the minority phenomenon (which operates here as elsewhere), but also because of the state of war and its dire consequences which continue to rage in the Near East.

On the other hand, the sentence that Jacques Doukhan quotes from Albert Memmi, which causes him obvious hurt—"The converted one is a destroyer and a traitor who deserves any and all punishments"—doesn't make too much sense here. Jewish extremists bent on the defense of Diaspora orthodoxy may appear to take such statements at face value. But in the eyes of most citizens of Israel the reality is quite different: Religious liberty exists here. Jews converted to Christianity may still retain total citizenship in the state of Israel. No one would think of inflicting on them "any and all punishments." On the contrary, some of them are entrusted with useful functions in the country, notably in an essential and continuing mediation between Israel and Christianity.

This change of attitude becomes all the more meaningful as the Pharisees continue to lose the monopoly they have held for 2000 years over the spiritual life of a people they succeeded in holding together during the corrosive centuries in exile. Israel, resurrected on her own land, has found again a pluralism which rejects the dogmatism and the unyielding doctrinal uniformity which were necessary during the Diaspora—a time when dangers from within and without threatened the very existence of the Jewish people. On the political plane, Israel harbors possibly more parties, opinions, and viewpoints than any other nation. In the area of religion, in the absence of a supreme magisterium, every Jew creates his or her own personal religion within the rich traditions of the fathers.

Therefore, a substantial portion of Jacques Doukhan's analysis applies to Diaspora conditions. This is very evident concerning the Jews, but it is also true for Christians. I have already pointed out that Christians are a minority in Israel. But that minority is in no wise monolithic. In Jerusalem thirty-three Christian confessions coexist without anything much in common, unless it be the fact they call themselves Christians. Their dogmas, their theologies, their religious rites, their cultures, their history, even their calendars vary. To step from one Christian church to another, the

11

observer must take a leap much more considerable than, for instance, to move from a Catholic or a Protestant church to a synagogue in Paris or New York City. In many ways, a coptic bishop and an American pastor, a Russian Orthodox and a South American Roman Catholic, strike one as less alike than if they had come from distinctly different religious worlds. Because of this modern situation, historical perspectives cast in the mold of exile times (pre-1948) are brought back again to haunt us.

Jacques Doukhan is right when, at the end of his presentation, he suddenly appears to be beset by a doubt. This is when he deals with one aspect of the problems he sets before us—problems, moreover, that run deeper and are more awesome than even he says. These problems really condition the total future of mankind, not merely our religious or spiritual future.

Rather than to persevere along the old-fashioned paths of classical apologetics, religions today, as Dr. Doukhan emphasizes, should apply themselves to measure the extent of past failures. No religious group has delivered convincingly what it promised the world: justice, peace, salvation, love.

Christianity, like Judaism, is no longer practiced except by a minority of the faithful; and the number of these faithful ones is on a steady decline. Judeo-Christian societies continue to be overrun by a neopaganism, whose idols are more deadly than those decried by the prophets in the days of long ago.

The Judeo-Christian world constitutes a minority in a total world community which appears content to drift toward the unspeakable possibility of atomic annihilation. Both Jews and Christians pretend to be the elect of God, the representatives on earth of the Master of the universe. Yet they have not been able to transmit their saving message to Asia, to Africa, nevermind the more and more paganized masses of Europe and America. In fact, Christianity since Constantine and Judaism since its hellenization have not been able to liberate themselves from the Greco-Latin ghetto of Hebraism where the essential events of their history took place.

The despair that Jacques Doukhan expresses in his Epilogue is justified, not only because of the Judeo-Christian drama (tragic but laughable), but also because of the common failure of Rome and Jerusalem, who appear today at history's judgment bar. The great conqueror is Babel, whose death-dealing legions seem stronger and more terrible today than ever in history. And the Molochs of modern times, whom we all serve too often, are no longer satisfied with the charred flesh of a few children sacrificed on their high altars; they demand and prepare for the apocalyptic sacrifice of

12

millions upon millions who, in the titanic blast of nuclear warheads, may perish in a cataclysm whose darkening thunderhead already overshadows planet Earth.

* * *

If there remains even an infinitesimal chance of survival for mankind, it can possibly be found in a reconciliation of Rome and Jerusalem. Jacques Doukhan seems to understand this. His quest takes him beyond mere theology and myth to a future aglow with hope and peace.

André Chouraqui

Foreword

I was greatly surprised one day when I received the manuscript of *Drinking at the Sources*; all the more so because I did not then know the author. My emotion and interest grew at each page, to the point where I was unable to refuse Jacques Doukhan's request to prepare a Foreword to his work.

I felt incapable of such a task for two reasons: any ability I might have does not lie in the writing of Forewords, nor do I believe in them. What purpose can they serve? Should they encourage the reading of the book? On that score an article in a newspaper, or a review, would certainly be more useful. Should a Foreword advise some sort of caution regarding the theses set forth in the book? My skills are not such as to enable me to do this; for my incompetency regarding an important aspect of *Drinking at the Sources* is total: the Talmud to me is a closed document. Therefore, only one option remains: to grasp the hand of the one who offers to guide me and to put full confidence in that guidance.

The reading of that portion relating to the Talmud caused me alternating feelings of surprise, amazement, and disquietude. By nature I distrust the best of apologies, for they may conceal a secret venom. I am also naturally fearful of make-believe analogies. I am less suspicious regarding the seventy weeks mentioned in the book of Daniel, since Christian tradition often has utilized (not to say tortured) these passages in Daniel.

I am slightly but not totally shaken, since I have read Jacques Doukhan with my normal aversion to research that leads too easily to rationalized constructions or conclusions. What I am saying is that I am in profound agreement with Jacques Doukhan's decisive conclusion on page 71: "Remarkably, the Gospel record does not give even one case of 'conversion' based exclusively on a rational demonstration."

15

Let none be astonished that I should linger somewhat on this word *conversion*. Dr. Doukhan's work must lead to a consideration of the subject. We Christians have maltreated, spoiled, and disfigured the word *conversion* to about the same degree as we have *charity*. And this has not been done by accident, since the beginning and the end of conversion is love. If conversion does bring one to a "break" in his life, it is to the end that he may love more. Conversion does not separate one from others when it leads one through the "narrow gate"; the convert above all else leaves behind what *he or she* once was. When conversion separates from neighbors and others, conversion has chosen the "broad way," where hardness of heart and bitterness of opinion have banished love.

Authentic conversion does not transform an individual into either a defense or prosecuting attorney, nor does it make of that individual an enemy of anyone. One cannot be truly converted against any doctrine or human community. If so, the "conversion" was merely a change of ideology, while the person remains as before, fed by sinful rivalry, competition, suspicion, and accusation. Such "conversions" fail to acknowledge the revelation of peace provided for mankind in the bosom of scriptural Israel.

One is converted for God and not against people. To be for God means to be in harmony with Him who would teach everyone the ways of love. Conversion does not lead one to criticize others but to change one's self into a person who chooses to reflect his God.

Conversion of the heart brings with it a conversion of the thoughts God gives us to serve Him. This conversion of thoughts is not to be confused simply with the taking of positions contrary to those that nourished us in the past and which our brethren of yesterday still profess. Such a "change" diminishes a living faith and transforms it into a purely intellectual mutation.

True thought conversion is not a reasoning by antithesis. Who can describe how much the Jewish Scriptures and the New Testament have been distorted by the promoters of antitheses? Who could ever measure the ill effects caused by logicians who reduce everything to dilemmas and discount the grace of God!

The authentic thought conversion of those who love God proceeds from unplumbed depths. It is an obedience that takes root rather than uproots. If there must be authentic breaks in thought conversion among the people of God, this does not mean that we must abandon the field that has hitherto enriched us, in favor of another. It means, rather, that we will act like a professional well digger. He is not content to judge merely the exterior appearance of the ground; on the contrary, he digs deep. So we must descend beyond the crust of recent traditions. We must master the deepest strata of our heritage, where we shall see again the full richness that God once deposited in the depths for us. Upon that deep, common heritage, both Jews and Christians, because of our infidelities, have heaped our particular kinds of scorn.

I really have touched only lightly on an area in which we still have a lot to discover. My remarks have been inspired both by history—an unfailing mirror of relations between Jews and Christians—and by the studies of Jacques Doukhan. In all this I hear a call to examine carefully our hearts and our thoughts, which examination will constitute on our part the most humble and truthful conversion to the Lord.

F. Lovsky

2 — D.A.S.

Introduction

A Cry

We are about to raise some questions which never fail to arouse the passions of men. This is so because these questions touch upon highly explosive concepts and feelings that have held two influential communities—Jews and Christians—in their grip for two millenniums. Even now as we write, these communities are facing these questions generally with implacable judgments, inflexible dogmas, and deep-seated prejudices.

Bewildered and seemingly beaten in advance, one attempts to muster fresh words and ideas only with the greatest difficulty.

The temptation is to cry out in anguish and frustration!

In the present situation we can distinguish the strange and eloquent likeness of the dog named Balak, whose tale is told by Agnon.[1] Balak, friendly and harmless, regularly stretched out on the streets of Jerusalem. A painter passed by one day and, prompted by unemployment, sadistic cruelty, or simply a bent for foolishness, painted on the dog's back the words "Mad Dog." That was the beginning of a frightful experience for poor Balak. The words stuck with the dog and settled his fate. He was chased, stoned, and banished from the city.

What was this terrible truth which everyone knew about him, but which eluded his ken? The dog no doubt surmised that the letters inscribed on his back had something to do with the distress. Unable to take any more, he wanted to understand. "So it was that again and again he turned his head to try to discover the evil truth. He turned and turned until exhausted, but his exhaustion was in vain: He couldn't read! Fatigue was followed by bewilderment. Everyone about him knew the truth he carried on his back; but he, the master of that truth, did not know what it was. He let out a prolonged howl of grief as if to ask: 'That truth, what is it?' "[2]

19

The dog Balak was painfully aware of the scandalous injustice of his fate. Balak could not read the label, so he was not bound by it. He was consequently placed in the very best situation to find the truth. Balak was the only one who could discover the truth, because he alone lived inside the only one really concerned with it and seriously affected by it.

In the same way, Jews and Christians, the one for the other, carry the burden of false labels. We witness the distress and unfairness of it and can no longer hold in the cry and questioning of our mind and heart. The question posed by Balak torments us. We long intensely for an answer. The truth which we seek concerns us personally.

As Jews we certainly are involved in this problem. In a very special sense it is our problem. Because of our Jewish status—the author's as well as Jewish readers—we must be considered secure in our search from any thought of conscious or unconscious anti-Semitism. We are thus immune to that hatred that so often, consciously or unconsciously, stems from it.

As both Jews and Christians, we believe we can proceed with even more stringent objectivity than otherwise would be possible in our inquiry into the origin and nature of that conflict which truly is like burning coals within our bosom. But the pain may be fruitful if we pose the problem in a way that will identify clearly the historical, theological, and human factors which brought the Church and the Synagogue to the parting of the ways.

It is very important that we know the truth that was entrusted to both the Jew and the Christian, in order that we can measure the distance covered, possibly the drift experienced, and the gravity of the misunderstanding that separates them.

It is very important for us to *drink at the sources,* so that at last, delivered from the intoxications of error, we might in some measure think freely, which is to think rightly.

The Problem

If the Jewish question is still posed today with so much sharpness, it is surely because it appears against a backdrop of passion and agressiveness. Conflict and opposition—in fact, a full-scale rupture—long ago gave birth to the current situation. The actors in the drama are characterized on the one hand as "stiff-necked" and on the other as "impostors." Meanwhile those involved "seem to work feverishly and as best they can at deepening the chasm that separates them. In this wise they exhibit an equal denial of the fundamental commandments of the God on whom they would claim a monopoly. The story is a very sad one, and without honor for either Church or Synagogue."[3] If all people were either Jews or Christians, there would be no Jewish question. The question arose in the wake of the bitter separation—when both stood off in total confrontation, hurling accusations and contempt in the name of their Truth.

Our first task must be to rescue historical fact from fiction in an attempt to discover what indeed was responsible for the schism. The matter is laced with uncommon complexity, because the separation did not come suddenly nor was it clear-cut. Of primary importance will be the identification, from each side's viewpoint, of the truly decisive factors and the arguments both sides have used in constructing seemingly insurmountable walls. Then we will be better able to define clearly the origin and the nature of the separation and to determine, in good faith, just what is involved in this age-long drama.

The Theological Argument

"The change from Saturday to Sunday as the day of worship . . . made a choice between the two imperatives. It is understandable, in the light of the change, that conversion to Christianity could appear to Jews as a denial of Judaism. This was a matter of conscience the importance of which I would not minimize."—Cardinal Danielou

The truly decisive factor separating the Jew and the Christian 2000 years ago was first of all theological. And let me say without delay that this separating factor was due to the initiative of a growing majority within Christendom. Very early Christians felt that emancipation from the Jewish background was essential, that it should be made crystal clear that Christianity was a "New Covenant" without any attachment whatsoever to what was termed the "Old Covenant." Separation from the original tree, even an uprooting, was considered of first importance. Christianity was not to be an extension of Israel.[4]

This theological necessity grew in importance as time went by. And it must be admitted that the work of evangelizing Roman pagans carried a serious handicap due to "Jewish" requirements and the Law of the Jewish Scriptures, which was still very much a part of the Christian's theology in the early years.

Separation came in Christianity when a major segment reacted against Judaism by rejecting its Law. It must here be made clear that by Law we are not referring to the cultic laws such as those set forth in Leviticus. Not long after the inception of Christianity, the Jerusalem temple had disappeared. The question that remained between the two religions could only concern a particular group of laws that did remain.

Among that particular group of laws, the Sabbath deserves the most attention because it became the focus of the Judeo-Christian controversy. It was really in respect to the Sabbath that the two communities took up their opposing positions, to the point where, in official Christianity, "sabbatize" was equivalent to "judaize."[5] In order to mark a complete distinction from Judaism, the majority of Christians thought it necessary to reject the Sabbath.

To be sure, earliest Christianity had no problem about observing the Sabbath. But the urge grew in strength to distinguish themselves from the Jews, and they chose to mark the new dispensation on the calendar, replacing Saturday with Sunday as the day of worship.

The change started timidly at the end of the first century, as is evident from this isolated remark by Ignatius of Antioch: "Those who lived according to the old order have found the new hope. They no longer observe the Sabbath but the Day of the Lord—the day our life was resurrected with Christ and by His death."[6]

However, at the time of the Marcionite heresy, in the second century, the Christian reaction to identification with Jewish customs became important. Thus Marcion ordered the fast on Saturday, justifying it in this way: "Because it is the rest of the God of the Jews, who has created the world and has rested on the seventh day," he wrote, "we fast on that day in order not to accomplish on that day what was ordained by the God of the Jews."[7]

The Christian reaction was reflected in the attitude of Bishop Victorinus de Pettau, in the third century, who did not want it to appear that he "observed the Sabbath of the Jews."[8]

The imperial councils of the fourth century were decisive. For the first time officially, due to the obsession not to be identified with the Jews, the observance of Sunday was made official by decree.[9] A case in point, among others, was the Council of Laodicea (held between A.D. 343-381, exact date unknown): "Christians must not judaize by resting on the Sabbath, but must work on that day, honoring rather the Lord's day by resting, if possible, as Christians. However, if any shall be found judaizing, let them be anathema from Christ."[10]

It seems clear, then, that because of a determination to disassociate itself from the Jews, Christianity rejected the observance of the historic Sabbath.[11] Nor was it by chance that all this came to a head in the fourth century—the century of Constantine and the time when the Church became the official religion of the state.

These two events are closely related historically. The Church became a power in the empire because of her marvelous ability to adapt. By rejecting

24

the so-called Mosaic Law and adopting Sunday as the day of worship (which was also a holy day for the Romans, who worshiped the sun[12]), Christianity greatly facilitated its task. Practically speaking, was it not better to discard the Sabbath in order to more freely evangelize the pagans? In the eyes of church leaders the Church would become much stronger.

But to open one door was to close another. By her rejection of the Sabbath, the Church was indeed more successful among the pagans, who could now be incorporated en masse; but by eliminating the major obstacle in the way of the Gentiles, the Church built a major one for the Jews.

With this open rupture under Constantine, the Church sealed its fate. Henceforth no real dialogue was possible between Christian and Jew. The Christian took his stand with Christ and heaped reproach on the Jew for rejecting Him; the Jew took his stand for the Law, as a means of justifying his refusal.

Whatever intrinsic value Truth might have, the Jew could not accept it unless it met the ancient criterion: "To the Law and to the testimony! Whoever will not speak according to this word, there shall surely be no dawn for him." Isaiah 8:20. Modern Language Bible. Every day the Jew discovered in the Law a definition of his role as a Jew. To reject that Law was nothing less than self-rejection, which was pure betrayal.

"If Israel does not accept the Torah, says God to His angels, you and I can no longer subsist."[13]

"The Holy One, blessed be He, covered the Israelites with Mount Sinai as with a cistern, and said to them: 'If you accept the Law, all is well; if not, there shall be your tomb.' "[14]

These quotations from the Talmud, which are all the more interesting because they date from the period of the separation, offer the Jew his self-defense.[15] "We can never abandon the Law," was the Jewish response to Christian proselytism. "You might just as well ask us to deny our being and our God."

The historian Jules Isaac agrees: "The Jewish rejection of Christ was triggered by the Christian rejection of the Law. . . . The rejection of the Law was enough: to ask of the Jewish people that they accept this rejection . . . was like asking them to tear out their heart. History records no example of such a collective suicide."[16]

One can understand from another angle how Judaism, emerging from the controversy with a recently born Christianity, could appear to the Christian historian as too law-centered. Did not the Law become the rallying point? "Why," asked Harnack, "did Judaism harden its stand within the Law?"[17] "Because," replied Marcel Simon, "the Law was the principal object of Christian assaults."[18] This simply is to recognize that the Law was the place and the reason for the Jewish refusal, which reveals, of course, a vicious circle. Judaism hardened its stand within the bounds of the Law because the Law was the principal object of attack—"principal," because this was the major point that separated the Jews from the Christians. Because of the Law rather than because of the Messiah, the Jews could not bring themselves to recognize Christianity's claim to fuller truth.

Even today, one of Judaism's most authoritative spokesmen, André Neher, states that the Christian's messianic concepts, contrary to what one would expect, are not what separate the Jew from the Christian. "A Jewish messianism carried to its ultimate consequences, is how Christianity appears, and the theology of this messianism could be a subject of alarm only for a Jew accustomed to mezzanine considerations. How many Jews with adventuresome souls, how many mystics among which one could name more than one serious doctor of the Law, have touched the frontiers where the border lines between Christianity and Judaism fade into unclearness as regards their resolve to remain true and faithful? We would say rather that they remained really true and faithful."[19] One could, therefore, in harmony with such statements, claim to hold the Christian conception of messianism without betraying the essence of Judaism.

Rather, as André Neher clarifies the point: if "irreconcilable divergencies" exist between Christianity and Judaism, they must be sought at the level of the Law.[20] Jewish contemporary theology continues to place *here* the point of separation. Judaism, according to André Neher, is the "Community of the Law." This is what characterizes it vis-a-vis Christianity.[21] Historically it is on this point that the schism was conceived.

One can expect to find traces of this fact in the current Judeo-Christian separation. The conflict over the Law is still the major element dividing the two communities. In rejecting the Law, the Church rejected Israel. The close dependency between the Law and Israel has been noted by many historians of Christianity. "The rejection of Israel by the Church beginning with the fourth century," says Marcel Simon, "is invariably a corollary to doing away with the Law."[22] Thus Christianity made it virtually impossible for Jews to listen to its message.

The historical record notes that Christian evangelism, which enjoyed enormous success up to the fourth century among the Jewish masses, suddenly stopped.[23] Israel, in terms of the Law, had been rejected by the Church; and her doors closed to the Jews.

One can hardly imagine what might have happened had the Church resisted compromise. The expansion of Christianity would have continued

26

especially well among the people of its origin. The faithful Jew would have accepted the Christian faith without obligation to convert to a new religion. The Jew today would not stand in a face-off with the Christian; for the Christian, by nature and in Christ, would be a Jew. In sum, the Jewish question and schism would not have existed.

But events turned differently; and now conversion, for the Jew, is equated with betrayal: first, betrayal of his God; then betrayal of his people. This betrayal is made acute by the fact that early Christian anxiety to be distinct from Israel gradually became agressive. Eventually, antipathy compelled Christians to persecute "these rebels against God." Anti-Semitism was born. The question was no longer one of religion or theology. The Jewish-Christian separation had become a full-blown human problem.

The Human Argument

"It is urgent that Christians cease once and for all to picture the Jew in stereotypes produced by centuries of antagonism. Let us eliminate forever and combat with courage in all circumstances those caricatured representations so unworthy of honest people and totally unsuitable for a Christian, such as these: The Jew is 'quite different from anyone else'— with a dash of scorn, even contempt added—the Jew is ambitious and conspiring and practices usury; and yet another more terrible in its consequences makes the Jew guilty of deicide. Such stereotypes can be termed infamous, though they still are circulated openly or by inference. We denounce such practices in any form." [24]

In our consideration of the Law as that point where the Judeo-Christian separation began, there was room for discussion and argumentation. But when we deal with the human consequences of the separation, free discussion and suspended judgment no longer make sense. Nor is it possible. We are no longer dealing with an idea—a theological opinion— but with a manner of life. Anti-Semitism is rooted so profoundly in mankind, has taken such a hold on mankind's subconscious, in addition to thoughts and acts, that it tragically has closed most human doors to the Jew. In a unique way, life for him is no open sesame.

Anti-Semitism does exist, undeniably. Sadly, however, few people understand the serious threat this monster represents. Some even doubt the monster's existence. One's own personal experience as a Jew underscores a daily anti-Semitism shot through with ill will and interlaced with absurd legends and tales—even in Christian minds. The situation seems incredible!

No matter how great public ignorance and indifference may be about it, anti-Semitism is a fact of modern life. And the disease is grave. However, before we can truly remove this evil, we must first understand what it is and what it does to us—both Jew and Christian. How did we get to the point where we now seem to be? Anti-Semitism had an origin, an evolution. Can the demon be exorcized? Obligation is laid upon us to answer these legitimate questions, because, if for no other reason, anti-Semitism continues to play a crucial role in the Judeo-Christian separation.

Anti-Semitism—Its Identity

The roots of anti-Semitism, consciously or unconsciously, lie deep in the historical subsoil of hatred, prejudice, and error. It manifests itself in two ways: (1) a rigid stereotype of a Jew built upon subjective judgments; (2) a particular theological construct regarding the Jew-Christian separation.

Psychological Anti-Semitism. Here is the source of those clever little smiles intended to say more than they do. Here, too, is the basis for an unfortunate vocabulary spawned by our current civilization which, by inflexible edict, sets the Jew in a concrete atavism (manifestation of primitive characteristics of a family or a race) from which he can never escape and which he can never understand because it doesn't make sense. From this source also comes "a portrait traced by others, in which the Jew does not recognize himself."[25]

Imagination has joined psychology to equip the Jew with a long nose, a special odor, and a full array of biological oddities.[26] Countless Christians have visited Israel and have been hardly able to conceal their astonishment that the reality didn't tally with the picture: very few Jews were found to have a long nose, wide flappy ears, etc. As a matter of fact, biological differences exist among the Jews just as they do among Christians. As with Christians, many different types of Jews exist: Chinese Jews, black Jews, Berber Jews, Hindu Jews, large blonds with blue eyes, small browns, etc. In point of fact, modern anthropology has exploded even the notion of a Jewish race.[27]

So the invisible, the unverifiable, becomes the last resort in the effort to spin fables on Jewish differences. There exists, it is said, a Jewish intelligence—praised and admired. This unique intelligence is said to be strictly Jewish and cannot become Christian! Jean-Paul Sartre has given a special twist to this contention. "Anti-Semitism," says he, "is an attempt to upgrade mediocrity per se, in order to create a mediocre elite. For the anti-Semite, intelligence is Jewish; he therefore can scorn it along with the other virtues the Jews possess."[28]

Yet this Jewish intelligence, along with the other apparent qualities conceded to the Jews, sooner or later will be turned against them: "Is it said that the Jew is intelligent? You might think that is a quality. But not at all! The Jew is TOO intelligent. His sagacity is destructive, corrosive, vexing."[29]

Nor can we forget the popular image often created to represent the Jew in Christian circles. This image depicts knavery, cupidity, wealth, and crass materialism as naturally Jewish. Though the image is legendary, it is still false. One can find just as many poor people among the Jews, if not more, than elsewhere. Of course, some Jews are rich, some are covetous, and some are deceitful, just as are some Christians. But in the case of the Jew, these faults are not individual weaknesses—they are *Jewish* characteristics. The difference lies in the community to which the individual belongs.

Literary works generally present the Jew as "deceitful and cowardly," but it was left for Albert Memmi to reveal the secret of it all: "Let none tell me that you cannot find deceitful and cowardly Christians. Such are deceitful and cowardly on the one hand but upright on the other, the same as all other people. Their deceitfulness and their cowardice are not related to their membership in a community. Furthermore, positive heroes are also Christians. The Jew practices usury and is cruel because he is Jewish."[30]

If one falls victim at the hands of a dishonest businessman who happens to be Jewish, the normal comment is the following: "He's Jewish—what can you expect!"

The anti-Semite monster must be pursued into the depths of his lair so we can denounce even his language. Yes, even the language people use can be sullied. "What a Jew," people often exclaim, though the person they have in mind may not be a Jew at all. He is called a Jew simply because he has shown cunning and avarice.

Large noses, flappy ears, intelligence, covetousness—the portrait of Jews being unlike other people makes a story without end. The image is always imprecise, out of focus, and varied according to the individuals, groups, and countries involved. Time and place also play a role.

However, one point is constant: whatever may be the Jew's quality or fault, even when such are found similarly among non-Jews, the Jew possesses his faults or qualities because he is Jewish. Yet the differences between Jews and Gentiles, in these areas, are based upon impalpable, unverifiable circumstances.

Nevertheless, as if to discourage in advance and foil any attempt to remove these false differences, they seem to have been given shelter under the thick fog of irrational, absurd thinking, where they cannot be successfully identified or ferreted out. No doubt Einstein was right when he concluded with sadness, "It does not make sense to try to convince others, by all kinds of deductions, of our parity, because their opinions are not rooted in the brain."[31]

This determination to be separate seems to have been implanted in the Gentile subconsciousness. A terrible mark has been placed on the Jew's forehead—that of guilt. The difference, therefore, is not only on the plane of psychology. Anti-Semitism, "the mystery of Israel," uses also the language of theology.

Theological Anti-Semitism. In speaking of theological anti-Semitism, we recognize the existence of Christian anti-Semitism. When this point is clearly made, a Christian reaction is to be expected; for the Christian will say with total sincerity that Christians cannot be anti-Semitic. Further conversation would then lead to the observation that "if the Jews have suffered so much through anti-Semitism, it is because—" Then follow explanations, theological justifications, and the "reasons of conscience" that sent Jews to the stake and the scaffold. Murder and assassination are also explained as unfortunate necessities.

In short, the Jew in all ages, and even today, is considered to be responsible for the death of God—this simply because 2000 years ago some of his probable ancestors could have sentenced Jesus of Nazareth to be crucified.

On one hand, accusations; on the other, pretended love. On one hand, anti-Semitism, is condemned; on the other, anti-Semitism is fed generously by theological reproach.

Yet a relationship exists between the two points of view. This was perfectly clear to Kierkegaard, who said: "Tell (to the child) the tribulations of Jesus during His life, the betrayal by one of His close companions, the denial by several others, the insults and revilings of others up to the very moment when they finally nailed Him to the cross, as you can see in the sacred pictures, asking that His blood fall on them and on their children, while He prayed for them and asked that this not be so, and that the heavenly Father would forgive their sin. . . . Tell how at the same time that Love lived, an infamous thief sentenced to die was preferred by the people who greeted his release with hurrahs . . . while they cried out: 'Crucify Him! Crucify Him!' in the face of Love. . . . What impression do you think that story will make on the child? . . . He will resolve firmly, when he has grown up, to cut to pieces the ungodly who acted thus toward Love."[32]

Kierkegaard's observation was confirmed on an Austrian television

31

program during a recent Easter season. A former Nazi, now "repentant," was interviewed. He explained how this indictment of the Jew had been taught to him repeatedly since his early youth and had contributed largely to instilling in him a hatred, even as an atheist, that would qualify him as a future member of the Hitler Youth.

Of course, not all German Christians fell into the snares of Naziism; many of them, even when they were anti-Semitic, battled this evil at the peril of their lives. Yet these same Christians who opposed the Nazi monster, possibly unconsciously and without understanding the consequences of their attitude, tried to explain, at least partially, the Jewish predicament.

Articles and publications aimed at demonstrating the fulfillment of certain biblical prophecies used the "Jewish argument." It went like this: "The predicament of the Jews is terrible, frightening; but could not this be a striking confirmation of biblical truth? After all, did not the Jews crucify the Incarnate God?" At times in the course of a public lecture, photographs were exhibited showing, with a touch of morbid zeal, such concentration camps as the one at Treblinka. Human bodies, even skeletonlike naked children, were pictured—all this with the implied message that, after all, here was irrefutable proof that the Bible is true and that God can be relied upon! "Impenitent theologians," commented Jules Isaac, "do not bring God into this; human villainy is enough."[33]

The worst is the trick this can play on conscience. Persecution of the Jews actually becomes the will of God; thus, one can be at peace in hatred as well as in indifference.

Furthermore, the deicide theory not only encourages Christians in their hatred and scorn, but it also provides an explanation of the Jewish refusal to listen to talk about Christ. "The more Christians insist on this accusation, the more obstinate Jews continue in their denial."[34]

How, really, could it be otherwise? Wearied with this accusation, that Jews killed God, the Jew finally begins to wonder if, after all, the death of Jesus were not justified; perhaps the Christ of whom the Christians talk did deserve death. Perhaps He *was* a traitor to the nation—a dangerous impostor. Often the Jews have taken refuge in that defense. Albert Memmi was not an isolated one: "I told the members of the school colony," he wrote, "the story of a Christ who was a traitor to His people and to His religion."[35] Thus, if Christ were put to death, the conclusion is that He was guilty. The Jewish denial owes much, it is believed, to this conclusion, which, in a way, is a reaction. Albert Memmi's further comment is still more enlightening: "Up in that small mountain village church, and be-

32

cause of my conclusion, I had just received a solid beating. Thus, for two thousand years Jesus has been, for the Jew, a pretext for continuous offence, fagging, and attack, in which he often has found death."[36]

To accuse the Jew of having crucified Christ is to force him to have defamed God. The deicide argument adds depth to the Judeo-Christian chasm.

* * *

Theology and psychology join hands to fashion the face of anti-Semitism. It is rarely possible to make a clear-cut distinction between them in their common enterprise, for they seem to merge confusedly one with the other.

In fact, a certain kind of theology feeds on anti-Semitic psychology. The hero of the Old Testament is given the trappings of the deceitful Jew. When the patriarch Abraham pretended that his wife was his sister, was he not answering the call of those deep character instincts imbedded in his race and culture, such as deceit? Because of such deep traits, he was willing to sacrifice to his personal interests the womanly honor of his wife.[37]

Were one to accept this view on Jewish atavism, could not one wonder why it did not appear similarly in the Jews of the New Testament? And were one to dare to pursue this question further, could not one wonder why this atavism did not show up, with its well-defined consequences, in the character of Jesus of Nazareth, the most Jewish of them all?[38]

So go the arguments. A psychology is undeniably related to such theology. If the Jews are to be held responsible for the crucifixion of Christ, we must expect them still to carry within themselves today that singular "chromosome" that predisposes them with Caiaphas to murder and with Judas to betray.[39] They must be dangerous and must be dealt with! Even when they appear as lambs, the wolf lies underneath the skin, ready to take over.

Whether the arguments are psychological or theological, anti-Semitism has built a seemingly insurmountable wall between Jews and Christians. This was not done in a day. There was a beginning, a slow beginning. Originally, anti-Semitism was only a handful of seeds that germinated, sprouted, and grew. But in time it became what we now know—a monster, which I have endeavored honestly to explain and to denounce.

33

The History of Anti-Semitism

From Jules Isaac[40] to Poliakov,[41] including Lovsky,[42] to mention only the principal authors who have written in the French language,[43] one can follow the genesis, then the fluctuations of anti-Semitism that have marked both Jewish and world history.

The problem of the beginning of anti-Semitism has been solved much too quickly and superficially by many Jewish and Christian theologians. Anti-Semitism, according to them, has always existed as part and parcel of Israel's sinister destiny. Therefore, Israel alone must be responsible for it—a reprehensible but convenient way for such theologians to wash their hands of the dirty business.

"One must be well aware," writes a Roman Catholic historian, "that anti-Semitism is a state of mind that preexisted Christianity, and for which Christianity is in no way responsible."[44]

"It is a great error," a Protestant historian categorically proclaims, "to attribute to Christianity a responsibility in present-day anti-Semitism, which is several centuries older than Christianity. It really is a pagan instinct which comes to life from time to time."[45]

As for the Jews, and with them some Christians, they see in anti-Semitism an indication of Israel's election. Thus, over the signature of Rabbi Meyer Jaïs, one can read: "Yahweh Himself chose Israel to be a messianic and theophoric people, thus making them the object of hostility before the world and the pagan peoples, long before the incarnation, long before the deicide."[46]

Lovsky, a Christian theologian, likewise interpreted anti-Semitism as "The shadow carried by the mystery of Israel among the nations . . . just as enduring as the role of Israel in the world."[47]

True, one must recognize the reality of what has been "pagan anti-

Semitism." History records it. But in its relationship to what we have known in the Christian era, it is understandable that Jules Isaac in particular was led to distinguish two forms of anti-Semitism. The sporadic persecutions that the Jews suffered at the hands of the pagans have little in common with the perpetual and systematic persecutions perpetrated in the Christian community. "Between the anti-Semitism thus defined and delineated as pagan and the Christian anti-Semitism that was to relieve it beginning with the fourth century," writes Jules Isaac, "there are more differences than analogies."[48]

The fundamental difference has been made very clear by Marcel Simon: "Christian anti-Semitism, due to the fact that it is sustained by the Church, takes on an official, systematic, coherent character, which was always lacking in pagan society. It is fed by theology and serves theology. . . . A further difference is that while pagan anti-Semitism generally broke out spontaneously and only exceptionally was organized and directed, the Christian brand had a definite goal: to make the Jews appear odious. And it succeeded by a methodology that proved to be infinitely more calamitous than did pagan anti-Semitism."[49]

When we add that anti-Semitism seems to be anchored in our very being and culture, we are tempted to believe that it has always been thus.

Yet historical fact cannot compromise with personal feelings and convictions. The facts *are* there! And they are unquestionable. This phenomenon that we know and have defined and to which we have given the name of anti-Semitism belongs unmistakably to Christian civilization or, more correctly, to that civilization which, born of Judaism, took by opposition to it the *name* of Christianity. For, as it must be continually pointed out, the evil took root in the great separation.

We have already noted the relation between the theological rupture and the matter of the Law in the fourth century—a separation begun by Christian initiative and sponsored by Constantine. Curiously, as noted unanimously by both Jewish and Christian historians, there appeared in the fourth century the first seeds of anti-Semitism.

"Most texts dating from that period [the fourth century]," says Lovsky, a Protestant, "confirm that, at that time, a tendency of disfavor toward the Jews stiffened and produced a corps of hostile doctrines which were nourished by the many mistakes and misunderstandings attributable to the Judeo-Christian rivalry." Among the most serious and violent texts, Lovsky mentions particularly those of Aphraates, Ephraem, Augustine, and Chrysostom. "It was then," he says, "that the deicide myth came to its own and was granted credentials of false nobility in Christian thought."[50]

35

Laborious and remarkable research done by Marcel Simon, a Christian historian, brought him to the conclusion that "the expansion of ecclesiastical anti-Semitism dates from the fourth century."[51]

The Jewish historian Jules Isaac came to the same conclusion: "When, by a complete reversal of the situation, the Christian Church had ceased to be persecuted and victoriously had become the State religion, which was some 1600 years ago in Constantine's time (312 to 337), Judaism also suffered a reversal, but in the opposite direction. Judaism until then had enjoyed legal privileges under the empire; now Judaism was soon to be humiliated, vilified, and brought low. Henceforth a close cooperation between the Church and the State [Christian] now produced a mutual-benefit system which included discrimination, vexation, and painful interdictions."[52]

Beginning with the fourth century and lasting into the twentieth century, anti-Semitism was to take all possible and imaginable forms. Not wishing to lose our way in a thicket of details, we shall group the facts according to three important waymarks:

1. The fourth century, wherein we find anti-Semitism's birth as parallel to the rejection of the Law, the first accusations of deicide, and the installation of the established Church; thus, the great and formal separation.

2. The eleventh century, a time parallel to the Crusades, wherein anti-Semitism became cloaked in violence, and a focus of acute economic problems.

3. The nineteenth and twentieth centuries, in which a new ingredient, racism (parallel to nationalist and pseudoscientific movements), was added to the traditional spectrum of anti-semitism.

In the beginning anti-Semitism was essentially anti-Jewish; that is, it concerned itself with religion and expressed itself only in polemics and apologetics. Initially it contented itself with rhetorical figures, and often delivered scathing maledictions on all who held to the law of Moses.[53]

With the end of the eleventh century, during the Crusades, anti-Semitism was to become, for the first time, "systematically," violent.[54] At the origin of the massacres perpetrated by the Crusaders there was nearly always the charge of deicide: "These Jews killed and crucified Jesus without any valid reason. Let us take vengeance on them and eliminate them from the bosom of the nations, so that none shall again remember the name of Israel."[55]

Not only was it a violent death that Jews received at the hands of Christians; they also received a much more terrible, deep, and enduring wound that has followed them to the present time: the characterization of the Jew as a man with the moneybag—a practician of usury. That was the period when this image of the Jew appeared for the first time.[56]

What took place at that time which so abruptly enriched the arsenal of anti-Semitism? Two factors played a role in producing this image. First, the cruel insecurity in which Jews found themselves encouraged them to change their possessions into a commodity such as silver or gold that could be easily concealed in case of danger. Inasmuch as money in those days was hard to come by, those who had it soon became lenders. Such was the position monasteries found themselves in.[57]

Finally, the Jews were now forced by the circumstances of survival to do what the Christians, in principle, were forbidden to do. Until then the Jews had listened to the counsels of Jewish tradition and its spokesmen. On the eve of the first Crusade, the famous Jewish commentator Rashi was still of this opinion: "Let him who loans at interest to a stranger be accursed."[58] But one century later the rabbis had to surrender to the inevitable. Wrote one rabbi: "One must not loan with interest to gentiles if one is able to earn a living otherwise. But at the present time, when a Jew cannot own either fields or vineyards to insure a living, the loaning of money to non-Jews is a necessity and is therefore authorized."[59] "In this sense," writes Lovsky, "medieval society forced the Jew at least to practice usury, if not to engage in business."[60] The fact remained that from generation to generation the only way to survive at all was by interest earned on money, a resource that consistently staved off violent death and expulsion.[61]

These circumstances created a Christian reaction of horror and repulsion.[62] The Jewish reaction to such persecution further stirred up Christian hatred and contempt, creating a truly atrocious vicious circle.

But in the thirteenth century a yet more profound movement crystallized; the Jew was to become within the Christian society a foreign element, and the ghetto was born.[63]

In the fourteenth century came the myth that the Jew was "the devil in person."[64]

The fifteenth and sixteenth centuries made him a "pest"[65] that had to be destroyed.

In the seventeenth century the word "deicide"[66] was reemphasized. From there it was not far to go to create in the Christian mind the concept of a "foul race," which found special attention in the pseudoscientific speculations of the nineteenth century.

In the eighteenth century, that century of light, it became possible for the Jew, for the first time, to experience a mild form of emancipation, permitting him to mingle with citizens in general. Manners and customs, religion, and even the garb,[67] that had to then distinguished the Jews, tended to disappear. The traditional Jewish difference, however, was forced to go inward "to become a part of their very flesh, as though Western sensibility required the certainty of a distinction which, if ever superficially effaced, could subsist in an invisible essence."[68]

Thus the nineteenth century witnessed the appearance of racism—a new form of anti-Semitism resulting from a combination of circumstances favorable to its development.[69]

The study of many languages, then in full stride, influenced scientists to make a distinction between Aryans and Semites. The next step was for the biologists to make this distinction (which originally was of language alone) into one of psychology and ethnology. The Semite and the Aryan (or Indo-German) were set one against the other.[70] The comparison was perceived as an advantage for the Aryan.[71]

This desire to place the Semites in disadvantage can be explained by the situation in Germany. The German people were still struggling to extricate themselves from the particularist and anarchist political system of the preceding centuries which had made of them an assemblage of the most diverse peoples. They felt that the time had come to unify the German spirit and nation. Part of that effort was expended in an attempt to define more clearly what a German was. The German had to be distinguished from the one they all recognized as the foreigner in their midst: the Jew. The situation became a confrontation between the Semite and the Aryan. In Germany, racist anti-Semitism became a national necessity.[72]

The German people seem to need this thesis as a basis for national unity. Too bad, then, if historical truth stood in the way. "Even though it could be proved that there never was an Aryan race in the past," said H. Chamberlain, who was one of the most fervent in accepting the Aryan doctrine, "there must be one in the future. For men of action this is a decisive point."[73]

Myth had supplanted truth; legend was right and history was wrong. Richard Wagner promoted this error in the very first of his writings,[74] going so far as to resurrect the ancient god Woden and identify him with Christ. "Woden (Odin), the supreme god of the Germans, has not necessarily given his place to the God of the Christians; he can be positively identified with Him. . . . For in him is found, as in Christ, the Son of God, this decisive analogy: he also died, was wept for, and was avenged even as today we avenge Christ because of the actions of the Jews."[75]

Aryan mythology fitted nicely into a Christian mold, including even the deicide idea.

Wagner, though a pagan, could not exclude a religious justification of anti-Semitism. For him, the Jews represented civilization's "bad conscience" and "the hare to be hunted." It is not astonishing, therefore, that in concluding his resounding pamphlet, "Judaism in Music," he suggests finally "the redemption of Ahasuerus—annihilation" as the only way to solve the Jewish problem.[76]

Nazi Germany skillfully took advantage of this pagan-Christian background, which served, in effect, as the womb of Nazism. Christian Lovsky recognized this fact: "The national socialist frenzy . . . was not born by chance, nor did it come up overnight like a toadstool; it took hold of nations that harbored deep within violent resentments. . . . Baptized Christianity harbored hatred for Israel. Neither the Greek Chrysostom, nor the Protestant Martin Luther, nor the Catholic Bossuet had the intellectual prudence or the evangelical charity to exorcize the demons of anti-Semitism."[77]

* * *

Anti-Semitism is chiefly an historical phenomenon, with a beginning and a development. It is important to understand this in order not to bow to theological temptations which seem to search for easy justifications. Anti-Semitism does not go back to the eternal night of time, coming into existence when Israel emerges, as a perpetual shadow over a people alone responsible for it. It appeared chiefly in the fourth century, with the great Judeo-Christian separation—that forced, arbitrary rupture; it developed by the Christian in systematic contempt and persecution and ultimately led to the unbelievable Holocaust of the twentieth century.

Julien Green's apostrophe cannot be heard with indifference: "It is useless for us to try to hide: we Christians, almost all of us, are responsible in degrees that vary mysteriously from one soul to another, according to the light possessed. And the suffering of Jesus continues night and day in the world. After being nailed to a Roman cross, He is persecuted in His race with unspeakable cruelty. One cannot strike a Jew without striking with the same blow the Man par excellence, the flower of Israel. It was Jesus they struck in the concentration camps. It is always He, and He never ceases to suffer from it."[78]

39

Conversion and Betrayal

"The converted one is a destroyer and a traitor who deserves any and all punishments."—Albert Memmi

The Jew may become atheist, Marxist, or even Trotskyist; he may even go so far as to make war on God, religion, and the people of Israel, joining with parties whose well-defined programs are anti-Jewish and anti-Israelite; he may become hippie, Palestinian, or even gangster, yet he will remain for all of that a member of the family. To be sure, the family will argue with him, try to change his mind, but never would it come to the mind of anyone to deny his Jewish status. He will retain respect for the fact that he *belongs* to the Jewish people. In the state of Israel he can request the privileges of Israeli nationality.

But should a Jew convert to and embrace Christianity, he creates a community scandal. His relatives and close associates simply will be horrified! Suddenly a chasm will appear between him and them that seemingly nothing can bridge. Communication henceforth is totally blocked. It will be useless for him to claim that all worship the same God and all descend from the same sources. The converted one still remains a traitor, a renegade to whom even Israeli nationality will be refused.

One must try to understand.

Beginning with the first centuries, and particularly with the fourth, the Christian religion appeared more and more to the Jew not just as a heresy but more as a form of paganism. That religion had gone so far as to nullify that which in Israel had always been considered to be "a light to my path,"[79] the standard par excellence, *the Law*. More still, Sunday, the holiday dedicated to the worshipers of the sun, had been made to take the

40

place of the Sabbath day that had been fixed by God Himself at creation and reiterated on Mount Sinai.[80] And what should the Jews think about the sheer "paganism made up of processions, carnivals, and merrymaking; and of the worshiping of gods in plaster of paris, of human bones and relics?"[81]

All of this forged and rooted in the Jewish mind the despised image of a Christian who seemed to be a close relative of the "goys"—those pagans of ancient times. To become a Christian was not a commonplace deviation, a harmless mistake; more seriously, it denied the basic values of Israel's religion—it betrayed Israel's God.

But there is still more. Christianity, we have seen, was born in separation. In fact, the separation gave it new strength to survive and develop. Only this rupture could give Christianity an open door to the pagan world and permit the solid establishment of the Church in the Roman state.

To be sure, the separation did not take place suddenly. In Christian as well as in Jewish circles the first tokens were present from the start of Christianity.[82] Not until the fourth century did the rupture become effective—officially and irreparably. The Judeo-Christian conflict arose chiefly from that open separation; the Church, therefore, must be saddled with the principal responsibility for it. Jules Isaac seems to have perceived this conclusion, since he finds in that fourth century the portents of the great persecution of the Jews.[83]

More than heresy, more than paganism, Christianity, though it shared common roots with Judaism, became for the Jew the sworn enemy of Israel. And this enemy received in the Jewish community, even within the talmudic era, the significant names of Edom and Amalek.

Christianity has caused too many victims in Israel for the Jew suddenly and serenely to consent to dialogue—still less to conversion. Christian cruelty, frenzied massacres, still resound in Jewish ears. The wounds are far from healed, much less forgotten. Will healing and forgetfulness ever come? The wounds are perpetuated and renewed by that tenacious, subtle, invasive anti-Semitism which ever carries within it the ferments of unpardonable genocide.

"Once again the cossacks attacked Poland, once again they massacred the Jews at Lublin and in the surrounding areas. Polish soldiers assassinated a large number of survivors. Then the Moscovites invaded the Eastern Province while the Swedes did the same in the Northern Province. That was a very troubled period. . . . Entire Jewish communities were able to breathe again: they returned to Judaism. What else could they do? Accept the religion of their murderers?[84]

Rather than a matter of truth, we are face-to-face with honor!

41

"One who is oppressed cannot adopt completely the values and the customs of the oppressor, even were they stronger and more beautiful than his, even though better than his, without forfeiting honor and the essential pride of a human being."[85]

The Jewish question presents itself here not just in terms of theology, but, more dramatically, in letters reddened with spilled blood—written in the depths of our humanity. The problem is much more a human one than a theological one. And whatever value Christian truth invokes, conversion for the Jew always means joining the ranks of the enemy—and what an enemy!

Conversion, we have said, is considered a betrayal for the Jew. A curious addendum to this observation from the viewpoint of the Christian is that the Jew often remains a suspect—a potential traitor. Drumont made this judgment: "A converted Jew is possibly one more Catholic, but not one less Jew." The statement apparently is so true that in more than one Christian denomination there has been long hesitation before sending a converted Jew as a missionary in Israel—and that hesitation still subsists. Could the obscure fear be that this insecure sheep of the flock might suddenly turn against the mission?

Should one be astonished at this? Christian wariness conceals the uncertain feeling that the conversion of a Jew may not be complete and trustworthy. Thus, under the suspicious eye of a not-too-certain Christian, can the converted Jew be sure of a totally serene faith?

Even as a member of the Christian community, the converted Jew experiences a form of anti-Semitism which, even when unconsciously manifested, always hits him in the same spot. Even as a Christian, the century-old heartache remains; and his deep-seated wound really never heals. Because of this the converted Jew, whatever the quality of his convictions, measures by his suffering the distance that continues to separate him from his Christian brother.

For nearly two millenia Jews and Christians have stood in confrontation—a dispute between people who never seem to hear or understand each other, in spite of the memory of so much persecution and death. Theology seems to have lost its credibility when placed alongside racist judgments, sardonic smiles, and countless crimes. The separation has witnessed the emergence not only of two distinct religions, but of two peoples locked in radical opposition. Not only are they enemies, they have differentiated themselves even on the biological plane. Judaism and Christianity became two distinct races!

And then to remember a time when to be a Jew and to be a Christian

42

designated just one religion, one Law, and one people! A time when to be Christian was to be Jew and, conversely, a time when the great separation, that none could have foreseen, had not begun.

That was the time when the teachings of Jeshua (Jesus) and His disciples were still remembered—and accepted.

In the Beginning:
A Jewish Messiah

Two elements of Christian doctrine seem to have triggered the Judeo-Christian separation: (1) the acceptance as Messiah of a person named Jeshua; and (2) the categorical rejection of the Law of Moses.

Schematically and traditionally the conflict is as follows: For the Jew, Jesus of Nazareth is an impostor. He is not the Messiah awaited and announced by the prophets of the Holy Scriptures. Nor does He fit in any way the conception of the Messiah held in Jewish tradition.

For the Christian, the Jewish Law has lost its significance and normative value since the Messiah came. Nailed to the cross,[86] that law has lapsed and can no longer be invoked as the touchstone of the covenant relationship between God and His people.

One cannot, therefore, be a Jew and accept Jesus, just as one cannot be a Christian while continuing to Judaize by observing the Law. Thus Jews and Christians invariably have marked their fundamental differences. For both, the two positions are absolutely irreconcilable, and any effort at compromise is denounced by each side as heresy or betrayal. It is unthinkable on either side to be at the same time Jew and Christian.

In the beginning, however, the problem was not so clear-cut. The first Christians were, according to the New Testament story, pious Jews, very committed to their roots and sources. Pharisees, doctors of the Law, Levites, and ordinary people of all persuasions and classes were able to accept Jeshua as their Messiah without in any way bringing into question their Jewish status. In those times one could take one's stand with Christianity while remaining attached to his Jewish origins.

"For I could wish that I myself were accursed," exclaimed one of them, "and cut off from Christ for the sake of my brethren, my kinsmen by race. They are Israelites, and to them belong the sonship, the glory, the covenants, the giving of the law, the worship, and the promises; to them belong the patriarchs, and of their race, according to the flesh, is the Christ. God who is over all be blessed for ever. Amen." Romans 9:3-5, R.S.V.

A respect such as this for spiritual roots is very significant. It is true that Jewish tradition, both written and oral, confirmed the Christian doctrine on the coming of the Messiah.

It is likewise true that in the original expression of Christian theology, nothing was taught that could suppose an eventual rupture with Jewish sources in the form of an abrogation of ancient Jewish Law.

This observation may be different from the general view on this subject. The consequences to this line of thought have deep implications. Therefore we must verify and conscientiously weigh the facts regarding the sources from which Judaism and early Christianity drank.

A Jewish Messiah

"He has come; he has said what he had to say; he has gone away. But his footsteps still resound in my ears."—Rabbi Menahem-Mendel de Kotzk.

One can hardly expect to bring up the question of the Messiah without resurrecting long-standing passions. The problem is a fiery one, for it touches very intimately the Judeo-Christian dispute. We have no desire to quibble and cavil in an effort to substantiate one or the other position. The vanity of such polemics must be evident to all. Our purpose is rather to understand what it was, in the first centuries, that brought so many Jews, and not just the least among them, to recognize in Jeshua the Messiah they had been waiting for.

Among the reasons these Jews put forward to justify their new faith, the scriptural grounds occupied first place. The Inspired Oracles provided their best arguments; they turned readily to the Scriptures. They found that this Messiah fit precisely the scriptural portrait. Thus, their message always carried the supportive words "it is written."

"Paul . . . [in the synagogue at Thessalonica] argued with them from the scriptures, explaining and proving that it was necessary for the Christ to suffer and to rise from the dead, and saying, 'This Jesus [Jeshua], whom I proclaim to you, is the Christ [Messiah]. . . . These Jews [at Beroea] received the word with all eagerness, examining the scriptures daily to see if these things were so." Acts 17:2-11. "Now a Jew named Apollos . . . well versed in the scriptures . . . spoke and taught accurately . . . showing by the scriptures that the Christ [Messiah] was Jesus [Jeshua]." Acts 18:24, R.S.V.

The exact mission to which Jeshua was to be committed, His identity, and even the time of His coming were confirmed in the Scriptures and the traditions. The Jews who accepted the Messiah from Nazareth had plenty, therefore, to justify their commitment.

A Mission With Risks

The duel. The first promises regarding the coming of the Messiah are recorded on the early pages of the Hebrew Scriptures. The author of Genesis first described the advantageous conditions in which Adam and his companion had been placed. The necessity for Adam to maintain a close relationship with his God was emphasized; on this obedient relationship would depend his happiness, his well being, and even his life. The slightest attempt to "liberate himself " from the divine Law would open the door to the dire results of evil, including death. "The day that you eat of it you shall die." Genesis 2:17, R.S.V.

Yet man disobeyed and separated himself from his Creator. Death was inevitable, as well as sorrow, until death came.

The tragedy of that drama focused on Adam's unfragmented nature. He was matter that breathed and lived. "The Lord God formed man of dust from the ground, and breathed into his nostrils the breath of life; and man became a living being [a being that breathes]." Genesis 2:7, R.S.V.[87]

The death that was to afflict him was to touch his total, unfragmented being; therefore, no part of his being would survive the penalty. Adam's despair was complete, as suggested in his behavior: Adam hid himself!

The separation was so great that communication with God was no longer possible. All he now could expect was death. Then, suddenly, hope pierced the darkness; this hope was the first messianic promise. God spoke it, and His message took the form of an enigma: "I will put enmity [conflict] between you [the serpent] and the woman, and between your [the serpent's] seed [posterity] and her seed [posterity]; he [the woman's posterity] shall bruise [shuf] your [the serpent's] head, and you [the serpent's posterity] shall bruise [shuf] his [the woman's posterity's] heel." Genesis 3:15, R.S.V.[88]

This prophecy of doom fell on the initiator of the evil deed; that is, on the serpent. The message to him was that a murderous conflict would develop between him and the seed, or posterity, of the woman. Now we must decipher this mysterious language of the prophetic oracle.

I. *The Serpent.* In biblical writings, as in the writings of contemporary civilizations in antiquity, notably of Ugarit, the serpent generally is associated with the power of evil. Often the serpent is pictured as in war against God Himself: "In that day the Lord with his hard and great and strong sword will punish Leviathan the fleeing serpent, Leviathan the twisting serpent." Isaiah 27:1, R.S.V.

The New Testament—the book of Revelation in particular—picks up the same theme and sees in the serpent the incarnation of "the Devil and Satan." Revelation 12:9, R.S.V. The book of Wisdom, which dates from the middle of the first century before our era, also does not hesitate to identify the serpent in paradise as the devil in person.[89] In the same way Jewish exegesis, both traditional and scientific, has always understood the mythical serpent. Talmudic exegesis, with Sforno as a typical representative, considers the serpent to be the "evil," the "seductor,"etc. The late Umberto Cassuto, a member of the staff of Hebrew University in Jerusalem, sees in the Edenic serpent an allusion to the "principle of evil," to the "enemy par excellence of humanity."[90] Evil, the principle of evil, and the devil were to be attacked and ultimately wounded fatally in the head by the posterity of the woman, according to the Scripture.

II. *The Attack.* The fatal wounding of the serpent results in the salvation of man. But this act of redemption could not take place without a risk. The passage also tells us that in the course of this conflict the posterity of the woman likewise would be wounded to death. This is the interpretation given by the best-known of Jewish exegetes, Raschi: "Thou shalt bite the woman's heel, and by that shall she die."[91]

The two deaths were to be simultaneous, as is evident from the Genesis text. The heel would be struck by the venomous bite of the serpent simply because it is the foot of the woman's posterity that would crush the head of the serpent. Moreover, the play on words in using the same verb *shuf* to characterize both attacks tends to substantiate this explanation. It is suggested, then, that these two actions, though one was a "bite" and the other was a "bruise" or "crushing," would come as the result of one act.

In killing the serpent the posterity of the woman would run the risk of death. The act would be a sacrifice.

III. *The Posterity of the Woman.* One would expect that the conflict would involve the woman and the serpent. But though the serpent was the object of the malediction, it is the *posterity* of the woman that he will have to battle. Who is meant by that posterity? Should this word be understood in a general sense, meaning mankind, or in a particular sense, meaning a specific person?

Opinions are divided on this point. Some see here an allusion to mankind, others to the people of Israel; still others, as shown by the Septuagint translation,[92] think this is an allusion to a specific man.[93]

Understandably, on the basis of this last tradition, there was no hesitation later on to consider the posterity of the woman to be the Messiah himself. Even to this day[94] a strong exegetical current in Judaism has conditioned the Jews to think of Genesis 3:15 in a messianic perspective. The Targums[95] of Onkelos[96] and of Jerusalem[97] both refer to the Messiah in their commentary on Genesis 3:15. Likewise the Zohar[98] mentions it, claiming that the passage refers to a "messianic period."[99] Were a doubt still to remain, one could consult an ancient "gematria"[100] which definitely associates the word Nahas (serpent) with Meshiah (Messiah). The two words constitute by their alphabetic composition the same numerical value of 258. The Messiah and the serpent locked in conflict finally merge in a simultaneous death. Thus, man's first despair was met with God's first promise—a promise of the Messiah's intervention, whose redemptive mission was set against a background of suffering and death wrapped in sacrifice.

The Victim

And here the vibrant words of Isaiah the prophet regarding the Suffering Servant should be recalled:[101] "Surely he has borne our griefs [sicknesses] and carried our sorrows [pains]; yet we esteemed him stricken, smitten by God, and afflicted. But he was wounded for our transgressions, he was bruised for our iniquities; upon him was the chastisement that made us whole, and with his stripes we are healed. . . . He was oppressed, and he was afflicted, yet he opened not his mouth; like a lamb that is led to the slaughter, and like a sheep before its shearers is dumb, so he opened not his mouth. By oppression and judgment he was taken away; and as for his generation, who considered that he was cut off out of the land of the living, stricken for the transgression of my people? . . . Yet it was the will of the Lord to bruise him; he has put him to grief; when he makes himself an offering for sin, he shall see his offspring, he shall prolong his days; the will of the Lord shall prosper in his hand." Isaiah 54:4-10, R.S.V.

The mission entrusted to this suffering servant was to save his people at the peril of his own life. Often in Jewish tradition the suffering servant was identified as being the Messiah of Israel and not Israel itself.

A passage in the Talmud[102] alludes to an old tradition according to which, because of Isaiah 53:4, the Messiah was to call himself a leper: "The masters [Rabbana] have said that the leper of the school of the Rabbi . . . is his name, for it has been said: 'He has borne our diseases and he has borne our sufferings, and we have considered him as a leper, smitten by God and humbled.' "[103] A characteristic invocation in the Midrash [104] refers to this same text: "Messiah of our justice [Meshiah Tsidkenu], though we are Thy forebears, Thou art greater than we because Thou didst bear the burden of our children's sins, and our great oppressions have fallen upon Thee. . . . Among the peoples of the world Thou didst bring only derision and mockery to Israel. . . . Thy skin did shrink, and Thy body did become dry as wood; Thine eyes were hollowed by fasting, and Thy strength became like fragmented pottery—all that came to pass because of the sins of our children."[105]

It is always the figure of the suffering Messiah that Midrash Rabbah depicts in connection with Isaiah 53: "The Messiah King . . . will offer his heart to implore mercy and longsuffering for Israel, weeping and suffering as is written in Isaiah 53:5 'He was wounded for our transgressions,' etc: when the Israelites sin, he invokes upon them mercy, as it is written: 'Upon him was the chastisement that made us whole,' and likewise the Lord has laid on him the iniquity of us all. And this is what the Holy One—let him be blessed forever!—decreed in order to save Israel and rejoice with Israel on the day of the resurrection."[106]

The Targum of Jonathan also interprets Isaiah 53 in a messianic sense. Beginning with the introductory passages, the identy of the Servant is made clear: "Behold, my servant the Messiah will prosper, be lifted up and made strong; so long did the house of Israel languish after him."

There is, you can see, important Jewish literature on Isaiah 53. From the Talmud to the Targum, without neglecting numerous Midrashim, a well-established tradition portrays the Messiah as a specific person and distinct from Israel itself. His vocation, chiefly redemptive, necessarily included suffering and death. This was a Messiah who would bear the burden "of sin" for others by dying in their stead; He would be a sacrificial victim—a "sheep that remained dumb" before His assailants, to use the words of the prophet Isaiah. The technical expressions used by the prophet recall unquestionably the language of Leviticus. Like the Messiah, the sacrificial animal carried the burden of the Israelite's sin. Like Him, the animal suffered and died in the Israelite's place. Like Him, the animal's sacrifice brought peace to the troubled conscience. In this sacrifice God drew near,[107] and conditions were met that were favorable to a dialogue and a relationship between God and man.

This connection between sacrificial rites and the Messiah also had the attention of the rabbis of the Talmud: "R. Eleazar said in the name of R. Josei: 'This is a halaka [a principle] that concerns the Messiah.' Abba answered him: 'It is not necessary to give instructions here on all the sacrifices of victims, for this is a halaka that concerns the messianic era.' "[108]

49

The Cohen

However, this sacrificial victim, which enabled the sinning Israelite to draw near to God, always had to take place through the mediation of the sacrificator or cohen (priest). He was in charge of the expiation[109] occurring in the daily sacrifice for sin, as well as that more extensive expiation for sin confessed and remitted at the annual Day of Atonement (Kippur).[110]

The two expiatory rites—daily and yearly—were identical. The only difference was that at Kippur the blood was carried beyond the veil that separated the holy place from the most holy place in the sanctuary[111] and was sprinkled on the kapporeth (mercy seat).[112]

We must not overlook the fact that this ministry was not without risk for the officiating priest. The possibility existed that he would have to pay for this audacity with his life. For this reason, little bells were sewn to the bottom hem of his robes so that, as he moved about, the tinkling of these bells would reassure the waiting worshipers that the officiant was still alive. The priest bore the sins of the people and because of this was threatened by death. One can well understand why the descriptive text included the words "lest he die."[113]

This ministry, which included simultaneously the roles of intercessor and mediator, predestined the cohen to be considered one of the antitypes of the Messiah.

In Psalm 110, David, the illustrious king, foresaw "a cohen for ever" (verse 4), whom he calls "his lord" (verse 1). Authority and power are given him (verse 2), and he is charged in the day of God's wrath to "execute judgment among the nations" (verses 5, 6).

The thoughts expressed are familiar to messianic language: justice, domination, the day of God's wrath. Messianism and priesthood were thus bound up together, as Jewish tradition made clear by recognizing the Messiah in the cohen of Psalm 110.

For the rabbis of the Talmud, there is no allowance for doubt. When Rabban Simeon ben Gamaliel compared the merits of Aaron the priest of justice to those of the Messiah, he concluded, based on Psalm 110:4, that the Messiah was the most precious in the sight of God. "I really would not be able to say which, Aaron or the Messiah, is the most loved: but as said in Psalm 110:4, 'The Lord has sworn and will not change his mind, You are a priest for ever after the order of Melchizedek,' so I must know that the Messiah King is beloved above the priest of justice."[114]

A Midrash who tried to understand the personality of Melchizedek was

50

led likewise to consult Psalm 110:4 and to conclude, "Who is he, this righteous King and savior of whom it is written in Daniel 9:24 that he will 'bring in everlasting righteousness?' . . . He is the Messiah King of whom it is spoken in Zechariah 9:9: 'Lo, your king comes to you . . . on a colt the foal of an ass.' "[115]

All this indicates that an important current in Jewish tradition saw the coming Messiah in the form both of a victim and of a priest. Such a contradition may surprise our scientifically conditioned minds, which may have difficulty with one person's being both victim and priest at the same time! But this was the meaning in the parable of the "duel" we found in Genesis 3:15. The person meant by the "posterity of the woman" was to be at the same time the priest who bruised evil and made expiation for it, and the victim who would die doing it. This double messianic function explains the reason why the Messiah speaks of His identity in terms of two faces.

An Identity With Two Faces:
Messiah son of Joseph and Messiah son of David

The two faces of the Messiah portray two opposites so great that some have reached the conclusion that two Messiahs must appear with different vocations. The one predestined to suffer and die has the humble bearing of a victim; the other, predestined to glory and eternity, has the majestic face of a king. A talmudic passage alludes to this difference. The Messiah is designated as son of Joseph when He is the victim and as the son of David when He is the king.[116] Later, however, Jewish writings generally[117] build a complete dialectic on this distinction between the two Messiahs. As time passed, this distinction became more precise. But in the beginning, the traditional texts tended to warn against this creation of a double Messiah.

Suffering and death were not the only destiny of the son of Joseph. The Talmud speaks expressly of the death of the son of David.[118] It is also significant that the Suffering Messiah portrayed in Isaiah 53 is identified as the Messiah King,[119] a title that designated specifically the Messiah as the son of David.[120] The Messiah son of Joseph also appears with the bearing of a glorious Messiah. "Ephraim [son of Joseph] Messiah of our justice, reigns over them [the people of the world]; treat them as good seemeth to thee."[121] The ministries of the two Messiahs therefore come together, often giving the impression of being merged in one. It becomes difficult to disassociate them, so much are they alike. This identity was emphasized in the Targum, which went so far as to compare them to "twin kids."[122] One can even wonder whether, in the thinking of the Jewish exegetes in that early time, this confusion on two Messiahs did not betray a

51

fundamental idea that there really was only one Messiah. A discussion recorded in the Talmud seems to indicate that the rabbis were moving in that direction. One involved in the discussion inquired as to what the name of the Messiah should be. All advanced their particular theses on the basis of a verse from the Bible: "Menahem son of Ezechias: A second King David will reign gloriously and eternally, or even the leper called to be humbled and to carry the burden of our sufferings and diseases."[123] The possibility of two Messiahs never appears in the course of the conversation. In fact, the discussions of the rabbis seem only to try to understand the composite figure of the Messiah, for the various names they give Him are aimed rather at disclosing some aspect of His personality. According to biblical and rabbinical word studies,[124] it was conceivable that one and the same person should have several names. To talk about a son of Joseph or a son of David did not necessarily mean two different Messiahs. Thus the Bible and the Jewish exegesis of it affirm the one-Messiah concept, in which merge the traits of two different faces—of priest and sacrifice, of king and leper. That such a conclusion was conceivable bears witness to a particularly bold messianism. At that point, to accept the risk of the incarnation thesis and make of God the Messiah, was only a step away. Was, indeed, this step taken?

Messiah Son of David and Messiah Son of God

Alongside the many passages that present a Messiah with human flesh and blood, the Bible and Jewish tradition offer us a wide spectrum of texts in which the Messiah is also Eternal God. But understand well what we are saying: in no way are we referring to a concept, common in Greco-Roman mythology, whereby a particular person, because of superior qualities and merits, is elevated to the rank of some kind of god. Note that it is not the Messiah who becomes God, but God who becomes the Messiah. This difference deserves to be underscored, for it is important: the direction here is descending, not ascending. The Messiah involves a revelation of God, not a human usurpation.

Biblical theology is based upon the fact that God broke into human history in order to come to mankind. "This is what is found at the heart of all thinking in the Bible," writes A. Heschel, the Jewish-American theologian. "The path toward God is the path of God, for the religion of Israel finds its origin in the initiative of God rather than in the efforts of man."[125] "The Bible is an anthropology of God rather than a theology of man."[126] It is thus that the Israelite of the Bible understood the process of his salvation. "Our Redeemer from of old is thy name," exclaims the prophet when face-to-face with God. Isaiah 63:16, R.S.V.

God is at the origin of salvation. It is indeed remarkable that all the biblical texts mentioning the Saviour (Mochia) refer exclusively to God. If then, as we already have seen, the idea of salvation is attached to messianism, one must expect that the Messiah is of divine origin, for, says God, "I am the Lord, and besides me there is no savior." Isaiah 43:11; see also Hosea 13:4, R.S.V. This "divinity" of the Messiah was understood by Jeremiah. On the eve of tragedy for God's people, the prophet in his anguish sees a glimmer of hope—ultimate salvation in the form of a Messiah bearing the name of God Himself: "Behold, the days are coming, says the Lord, when I will raise up for David a righteous Branch [Tsemah]. . . . And this is the name by which he will be called: 'The Lord is our righteousness.' " Jeremiah 23:5, 6, R.S.V.

Looking beyond the immediate historical application to the return from Babylonian captivity,[127] Jeremiah is thinking, by analogy, of messianic redemption. So many indications make this very clear. Nor did this fact escape the attention of traditional Jewish exegesis, in which there is a consensus to interpret the text in a messianic sense.

"The Messiah," says the Talmud, "will have the name of the Holy Blessed one.[128] . . . For it is said in Jeremiah 23:6: And this is the name by which he will be called: 'The Lord is our righteousness.'"[129]

"What is the name of the Messiah King?" asks the Midrash. R. Abba ben Kahana says: "Yahweh is his name as written in Jeremiah 23:6, 'This is the name by which he will be called: "The Lord [Yahweh] is our righteousness." ' "[130]

The Targum of Jonathan fits the typical traditional view, since it translates the text in this manner: "Behold, the days are coming, says Yahweh, when I shall bring forth to David the Messiah of justice. He will reign as King and prosper. . . . And behold the name that he shall be given: 'Justice will be given to us in those days in the name of Yahweh.' "[131]

The Messiah of Israel thus is likened to God and bears the name (Yahweh) of God. But the identity is not limited to the name: the identity includes common attributes, such as their eternity and their royalty.

I. *The Eternal Messiah.* We already have found in Psalm 110, which is demonstrably messianic, these words: "You are a priest for ever."

The prophet Micah says of the Messiah that "his origin goes back to the distant past." Jerusalem Bible. Numerous passages in the Midrash and the Talmud bring the Messiah and God together in their eternity and make Them both the "firsts." "I shall manifest myself the first, as God . . . and I shall bring to you the 'first,' and that is the Messiah."[132]

Among the most clearly messianic passages in the Scriptures is certainly the ninth chapter of Isaiah, where the prophet describes the coming of an era of "peace without end." To the Messiah the inspired author gives, among other titles, that of "Everlasting Father."

Commenting on Isaiah 9:6, the Targum clarifies still further the divine attributes of the Messiah: "The prophet says to the house of David: A master teacher has been born to us, a son is ours; he will take the law upon himself and will set a guard over it; since the beginning his name has been pronounced: Wonderful in counsel, Mighty God, Everlasting One, Messiah during whose days peace will abound upon us."[133]

II. *The Messiah King.* This is the most usual messianic figure used in the Bible and in tradition. The patriarch Jacob, on his deathbed, instructed his children on the royal line of the one to come—he who would "take all nations out to pasture." "The scepter shall not depart from Judah, nor the ruler's staff from between his feet, until he [Shiloh] comes to whom it belongs; and to him shall be the obedience of the peoples. Binding his foal to the vine and his ass's colt to the choice vine, he washes his garments in wine and his vesture in the blood of grapes; his eyes shall be red with wine, and his teeth white with milk."[134] This Shiloh,[135] in whom Jewish tradition unanimously sees the Messiah,[136] belonged to the tribe of Judah. Rabbinical literature regularly calls Shiloh the "son of David," the "lion of Judah," the "Messiah King." Because of His origin He is predestined to reign. More than an Israelite royalty is involved here. Shiloh was to be anointed to rule over all peoples. A universal sovereignty is meant.

Psalm 2, which tradition usually places in the messianic category, also alludes to this particular quality of the Messiah.[137] The Talmud contains this ancient commentary: "As for the Messiah son of David, . . . the Blessed Holy One will say to him: Ask me something and I will give it to you, because it is said: Ask of me, and I will make the nations your heritage [Psalm 2:8]."[138] The Messiah, therefore, is the King of kings, the Lord of lords. But is not this a divine prerogative? Indeed, and that is why this extraordinary gesture on the part of God made a real impression on the doctors of the Midrash: "A king of flesh and blood permits no one to put the crown on his head; but the day will come when the Holy One, blessed be he, will place his crown on the head of the Messiah King."[139] That God and the Messiah should have in common royalty and eternity cannot fail to astonish, because this implies a similarity of nature. The likeness between the two is complete when we learn of their common identity of "spirit." The Messiah possesses the Spirit of God. On this basis Isaiah rests the Messiahship of Jesse's shoot: "There shall come forth a shoot from the

54

stump of Jesse, and a branch shall grow out of his roots. And the Spirit of the Lord shall rest upon him."[140]

Starting with this passage, the Midrash was led to discern in the first words of the story of Creation a shadow of the Messiah: "Genesis 1:2: 'The Spirit of God was moving over the face of the waters' indicates that the spirit of Messiah King was present, as written in Isaiah 11:2: 'The Spirit of the Lord shall rest upon him.' "[141]

God and the Messiah, therefore, are one and the same person. This, at least, is what one can deduct from the several best-known and least controversial passages we have chosen from the Bible, along with the traditional Jewish comments on them.

Furthermore, this Messiah, who has in common with God the vocation of a Saviour, access to eternity, the supreme royalty, the same name (Yahweh), and the same Spirit of God, is also the son of David, the shoot of Jesse. Such are the facts in the case. That which has become seemingly irreconcilable was once perfectly admissible in Jewish thought. The Midrash even undertook to explain it by an extraordinary hypothesis involving a mysterious seeding and conception from on high: "The Redeemer that I shall bring forth one day will be without father, as it has been said: Behold a man whose name is seed[142] and he shall germinate by his own means even as Isaiah has said: He rose up before him even as a seed, as a shoot that comes forth from dry land. . . . And it is of him that the Scripture says: 'Behold, this day have I begotten thee.' "[143]

Another Midrash, resorting to the same imagery, refers to the incarnation phenomenon in a yet more suggestive way: "Psalm 85:12. Truth will germinate from the ground. . . . R. Yudan says: It is our salvation that will germinate from the ground by the direct intervention of God. . . . And why does he say that it will germinate and not that it will be born? Because the nature of its birth will not be similar to that of earthly creatures, but will be different in all respects. . . . None will be able to give the name of the Messiah's father, and much less know it. This will be a mystery for all peoples until he comes and reveals it."[144]

Hebrew thought customarily uses paradoxes and takes delight in arriving at truth by bringing together seemingly irreconcilable elements. Typical is the truth regarding the double identity of the Messiah: glorious and humble, divine and human.

We find this truth in the writings of Jewish tradition as well as in the Hebrew Scriptures. And it is often found in the well-balanced verses of Hebrew poetry, of which Micah's song and its name combinations are deserving of attention.

Parallelism is without doubt the literary form which was greatly pre-ferred by Hebrew poets.[145] In a Messianic meditation, Micah the prophet gives us a perfect example of this type of expression. He spreads it over two chapters.[146] The presence of common themes and stylistic forms in both chapters confirms the type and invites a synchronized reading.

Micah 4:8-14   Micah 5:1-4

The Theme of a City

Jerusalem, kingdom, glory, power: "And you, O tower of the flock, hill of the daughter of Zion, . . . the kingdom of the daughter of Jerusa-lem." (verse 8)

Bethlehem, humility, smallness: "But you, O Bethlehem Ephrathah, who are little to be among the clans of Judah." (verse 2)

The Theme of Ancient Days and Dominion

In the end: "To you shall it come, the former dominion shall come." (verse 8)

In the beginning: "From you shall come forth for me one who is to be ruler in Israel, whose origin is from of old, from ancient days." (verse 2)

The Theme of Childbirth

Birth pains, anguish, and captivity: "Now why do you cry aloud? . . . Has your counselor perished, that pangs have seized you like a woman in travail? Writhe and groan, O daughter of Zion, like a woman in travail; for now you shall go forth from the city . . . ; you shall go to Babylon." (verses 9, 10)

Birth, deliverance, and return: "Therefore he shall give them up until the time when she who is in travail has brought forth; then the rest of his brethren shall return to the people of Israel." (verse 3)

The Theme of Divine Salvation

At war: "There you shall be rescued, there the Lord will redeem you from the hand of your enemies. Now many nations are assembled against you. . . . I will make your horn iron and your hoofs bronze; you shall beat in pieces many peoples." (verses 10-13)

At peace: "He shall stand and feed his flock in the strength of the Lord, in the majesty of the name of the Lord his God. And they shall dwell secure. . . . And this shall be peace." (verses 4, 5)

56

The Theme on Israel's Leader (The Messiah)

In humiliation:
"With a rod they strike upon the cheek the ruler of Israel." (chapter 5:1)

In glory:
"Now he shall be great to the ends of the earth." (verse 4)

The juxtaposition of the two chapters reveals the antithetical parallelism that characterizes them. On a given theme, each chapter proceeds to draw a picture of opposites. One can also see a play on parallels where the beginning of a paragraph parallels the end of another, and conversely, as pictured below:

Jerusalem, glory, might (4:8)   Bethlehem, humility (5:2)
Humiliation of Messiah (5:1)   Glorification of Messiah (5:4)

Such parallelism is of the chiastic type, so called because of its relationship (as pictured) to the Greek letter X (chi).

We chose these two chapters from Micah chiefly because of their Messianic character; Jewish tradition did not fail to see in them a clear allusion to the Messiah.

Thus, in Micah 5:2 the rabbis of the Talmud concluded that the Messiah would come from Bethlehem.[147]

Similarly, the judge (or ruler) mentioned by Micah (chapter 4:3 and chapter 5:1) is seen by the Midrash to be the Messiah.[148]

As for the Targums, the translation makes it clear that the Messiah is meant in both cases.[149]

If then, as recognized by the Jewish tradition,[150] these passages are messianic, it is more than interesting that the figures used are portraying glory and might as well as humiliation and suffering—the double identity of the Messiah.

Jerusalem—The Message of the Name

Jerusalem's name has been the subject of considerable comment in Jewish tradition. Midrash Rabba deducted from its etymology that Jerusalem resurrected images not only of the sacrifice of Isaac but also the personality of the priest-king Melchizedek.[151]

André Neher has noted, "The name of Yerushalayim is composed of the root *yaro,* that one finds in Moriah—the name of one of the hills on which the city was built, and of a second root, *shalem.* (In the Bible the name that the oral tradition uses is pronounced Yerushalayim, but is spelled Yerushalem.) It was on Mount Moriah that Abraham prepared the sacrifice of Isaac. Shalem was the residence of Melchizedek. David brought together in Jerusalem the memory of the sacrifice of Isaac and that of the pious Canaanite king Melchizedek."[152]

What these two men wrote is correct, but there is much more. An analysis of the name of Jerusalem reveals a number of remarkable theological ideas.

The "yeru" in Jerusalem etymologically recalls Mount Moriah, where an angel stopped the fatal stroke of Abraham's sword.[153] But Moriah was also the place where, according to the biblical story, God stayed the angel's sword in the punishment of David's troops.[154] It was, in fact, this event that determined David's choice of this site for the temple at Jerusalem.[155]

Significantly, Moriah appears in the Bible in only these two instances. It would seem that the Bible wanted to attach firmly to this site the idea of the saving intervention of God.

By choosing Moriah as the place where the Levitical rites would be performed, David indicated that a close correlation existed between the saving act of God and the ritual service in the sanctuary.

The "Salem" of Jerusalem evokes Melchizedek. The first time Salem is mentioned is in connection with him. Genesis 14:18. Melchizedek means "king of justice." He joined the functions of king (of Salem, that is, of peace) with that of priest (Abraham gave him the tithe and received a blessing from him). He also was called a priest "for ever." Hebrews 5:6. One can easily understand, therefore, the prestige that Jewish tradition accorded him as priest-king. Tradition saw in him generally an antitype of the Messiah,[156] identifying him, according to Philo's language, with the "Eternal Logos."[157]

In Jerusalem were associated the priest and the victim, the king and the obedient son. The saving intervention of God to bring justice and peace is also suggested. What more could be needed to make the deduction that the name of Jerusalem is an allusion to the Messiah?

The Bible authorizes this conclusion. Speaking of the New Jerusalem—a kingdom in which justice and peace will reign (the Messianic Jerusalem)—Jeremiah confers the name of "Yahweh Our Justice." Jeremiah 33:16. He confers the same name on the one he calls the Messiah son of David. Jeremiah 23:6.

Under the influence of these verses from Jeremiah, John, in the book of Revelation, associated the New Jerusalem and "my [God's] own new name." Revelation 3:12. Jerusalem and the Messiah, in their names, share a common message.

Using this same passage from Jeremiah, the Talmud and the Midrash place Jerusalem and the Messiah in a common order of ideas. "Do they not both bear the name of the Holy One blessed be he?"[158] It was to be expected, then, that the traits of the one, the Messiah, would be mirrored in the other, Jerusalem.

The Bible has taught us to lend attention to proper names, for often they have a definite message for us. Sometimes the message is found in their semantics and their phonetics. Always the aim is to communicate a warning—a prophecy. It is thus in names of God, of persons, and of places. In Micah 1, for instance, the prophet is pleased to find a divine oracle in considering the names of cities (Gath, Akho). Thus Akzib (Micah 1:14) which contains the root KZB (a lie), was to become the City of the Lie. The name of the Valley of Jezreel will be invoked to announce an impending historical event—an event similar to the one that took place there several centuries earlier. Remarkably, that reference was emphasized in the naming of the son of Hosea, who carried this geographical name in order to mark the similarity of two events in biblical history.[159]

The ancient saying that "Nomen est omen" (a name is an omen) must have been in the minds of the biblical authors and rabbis when they were dealing with the name of Jerusalem. The city bore such a halo of religious and political glory that her etymology could inspire a total spectrum of Messianic revelations. The name spoke of the Messiah's contradictory ministry. Once again boldness of thought made it possible to bring together irreconcilable ideas: Priest and victim, Everlasting King and a sacrificial son.

When one considers these two contradictory aspects of the Messiah, one could be tempted to think that Jewish tradition, nourished on the Holy Scriptures, imagined two Messiahs: the son of Joseph—humble, suffering, who died a voluntary, sacrificial death; and the son of David—covered with glory, royal, who will live eternally. Yet, we have been able to verify to what extent that distinction was artificial: the two Messiahs merged and focused in one person, the son of David.

But at the same time that this theme became clear and strong, another concept became real, even troublesome, for it brought everything back into question—the concept of the "Son of God." The core of the difficulty was this: Though it is permitted to be the son of Joseph and the son of David at the same time, it was impossible to be the son of David and the son of God at the same time. One is either son of man or son of God—not both!

But this paradox does not seem to have been unthinkable to the rabbis of ancient times. Serenely, they dared to propose this thought as though it flowed normally from the source. Could it be that the problem escaped them? Or that, enraptured with pure lyricism, they lost their sense of logic?

Not at all! They searched diligently and faced the risks and surprises that a diligent search must involve. Men of faith they were too, with the seeming irrationality and questions that faith itself engenders in onlookers. Completely committed to God, they had learned to recognize His acts in a long history saturated with messianic hopes. They were preoccupied little with the nature of the One who could save them; their primary interest was in the fact of their salvation.

The contradiction did not, therefore, hold them back. They continued their forward course to find the Messiah. Sometimes they saw Him with a scepter in His hand, every whit a king bedecked with a divine majesty—in the wake of Jerusalem; sometimes He came to them humbled and tortured by human suffering—in the wake of Bethlehem.[160] Had not the Bible announced two comings of the Messiah? Humble and seated on an ass, He would come as a man beset with earthly contingencies; gloriously riding the clouds, He would descend as a God with all power. Zechariah 9:9; Daniel 7:13.

60

The contradiction between the two comings is obvious. A certain teacher of the Talmud, after submitting this enigma to his disciples, put forward his own solution: "If they [all people] are worthy, the Messiah will come in the clouds of heaven; if they are not worthy, He will come modestly seated on an ass."[161]

That attempt to resolve the difficulty attests, at least, that in Israel the Messiah was represented in these two manners.[162] Does this mean that two Messiahs were expected? It never came into the mind of the rabbi to make two of one Messiah. He was forced into a compromise: the Messiah Himself would choose between the two forms, according to the moral state of man. His hypothesis had the merit of taking into account both biblical prophecy and logic.

But no such mental gymnastics are required. One could simply suppose that there would be two comings of the Messiah at two different historical periods. In this way, the problem of contradiction would be solved and the facts of the scriptural texts would be respected. If the Messiah were to come in two different ways, they would have to be two different comings: first, as a man of suffering, humble, seated on an ass, sent to His death because of us and for us—an expiatory sacrifice, within the time of mankind, in history; a second coming as a glorious and just God, a supreme King, in the clouds of heaven, which would necessarily imply a coming at the end of human time and at the setting up of the real City of God.

The second coming is beyond our intelligence. It is bigger than man's puny thinking. It belongs to God's time. It therefore can never be determined or realized through any human calculation.

The first coming, on the contrary, belongs to our history, fits our times and our measurements. One can readily understand that, belonging to the human order of things, this first coming can be situated in history.

A Coming On Time

To be sure, the Messiah must come in glory, "in the clouds of heaven," charged with a cosmic and definitive mission to bring about "the end of time." But He must, before this, come within "time," "seated on an ass," to accomplish the earthly and humble aspects of His mission.

The coming of a Messiah whose tragic destiny involved suffering and death implies necessarily a period of waiting in history.

We have seen that the ministry of this suffering Messiah—to "make many to be accounted righteous" (Isaiah 53:11)—recalled the expiatory efficacy of the Levitical sacrifice. How, then, could one not take note of a curious passage in Daniel's book, where it is the subject of expiation, and justice is related to a Messiah who is destined to be "cut off"?

"Seventy weeks of years are decreed concerning your people and your holy city, to finish the transgression, to put an end to sin, and to atone for iniquity, to bring in everlasting righteousness, to seal both vision and prophet, and to anoint a most holy place. Know therefore and understand that from the going forth of the word to restore and build Jerusalem to the coming of an anointed one, a prince, there shall be seven weeks. Then for sixty-two weeks it shall be built again with squares and moat, but in a troubled time. And after the sixty-two weeks, an anointed one shall be cut off, and shall have nothing; and the people of the prince who is to come shall destroy the city and the sanctuary. Its end shall come with a flood, and to the end there shall be war; desolations are decreed." Daniel 9:24-27.

This prophecy appears to indicate a precise date for the coming of the announced Messiah. The implication is important and must be looked at with due respect for the rules of prophetic interpretation. We must apply proper exegesis in order to make sure of the truth. This means, of course, that the language, context, and literary structure, as well as biblical and Jewish hermeneutics, will be taken into account.

The Context. The very first words of Daniel's chapter 9 indicate a specific historical context: the first year of Darius (538 to 537 B.C.). At that time Daniel, a Jewish prince in exile who had become a high official at the court of Babylon, was perplexed regarding the end of his nation's captivity, which had lasted for nearly seventy years. Daniel consulted the book of Jeremiah, from which he learned the number of years that "must pass before the end of the desolations of Jerusalem, namely, seventy years." Daniel 9:2. Because the end of the captivity was approaching, Daniel's anxiety is understandable.

The introduction (verses 1-4), like the conclusion (verses 20-27), mentions the same concern for time and refers to the same number of years (seventy). Both passages, which constitute the framework of the chapter, convey Daniel's preoccupation for the salvation of Israel. But between the two, Daniel inserts a prayer which reveals his basic concern: He is tormented by the thought of his people's sin, which he relates to the exile. Verses 5, 7, 16.

Daniel therefore cries to God, asking Him in mercy to intervene and forgive. He pleads that Jerusalem—and thus the sanctuary—be restored to its former glory and significance. (Compare verses 17-19.)

In answer to this prayer of "confessing my sin and the sin of my people Israel, and presenting my supplication" (verse 20), God sent an answer by the angel Gabriel.

"At the beginning of your supplications a word went forth, and I have come to tell it to you, for you are greatly beloved." Verse 23.

So Daniel's concerns and preoccupations became the points on which God answered him.

Was Daniel preoccupied by the sin of the people? God's answer was that in time sin would be expiated once and for all and eternal justice made secure. Verse 24.

Was Daniel concerned for the destiny of Jerusalem? God answers that in time a decree will be promulgated favoring the reconstruction of the city; yet, in later times, Jerusalem would be again devastated and destroyed. Verses 5, 26.

If in this same vision one sees the announcement of the coming Messiah, it lies in God's two answers.

First, we recognize the role of the Messiah in the expiation of sin. The manner in which this role is announced is significant. "Know therefore and understand" (verse 25) indicates that this role is directly connected to the first act of the vision concerning expiation. In other words, the coming of the Messiah clarifies the allusion in verse 24 to the expiation of sin and to eternal justice.

Then we must establish a point in history from which to calculate the time period leading to the coming and the death of the Messiah. Details relating to the destiny of Jerusalem will reveal that point. Verses 4, 25, 26.

The first words of the prophecy give us our clue: "Seventy weeks of years are decreed concerning your people and your holy city." The vision opens two shutters: The first points to the people and speaks of expiation and salvation; the second opens on the Holy City Jerusalem. This view concerns space and history and speaks of construction and destruction. Both are included in one time period: seventy weeks.

Daniel's prayer was in behalf of his people and of Jerusalem. It was to be expected that Gabriel's message, speaking for God, would deal with these two items.

The Literary Structure. When one considers this section of Scripture from a strictly literary point of view, one is impressed with a double emphasis: people and their sins, and Jerusalem and its sanctuary. Literary parallelism[163] suggests this form beginning with the prelude:

A Full Seventy Weeks Decreed	And Your Holy City
Concerning Your People	
To finish the transgression	To bring in everlasting
To put an end to sin	righteousness

63

To atone for iniquity	To seal both vision and prophet
	To annoint a most holy place
	(verse 24)

The two subjects of Gabriel's response to Daniel are announced in advance: "your people and your holy city."

The first three verses, in the Hebrew, are set to rhyme with two words each. All three verses deal with the people theme. The thought pattern concerns sin and forgiveness—items that Daniel's prayer dealt with in connection with the people. Verses 5, 7, 16.

The three following phrases in Hebrew, are set to a three-word rhythmical pattern and relate to the holy-city theme and the sanctuary. The thinking is entirely people centered, emphasizing such characteristic ideas as eternal justice, anointing, the most holy place, etc.

Then, a further parallelism exists between the verses themselves: the second element extends and completes the first:

"To finish transgression" is parallel to "to bring in everlasting righteousness." The end of transgression results in the reign of righteousness, or justice.

"To put an end to sin" is a parallel of "to seal both vision and prophet." The word KHTM (to seal) is used in both cases.[164] Thus the "sealing" of the vision or prophecy (that is, its fulfillment) is parallel to the "sealing" of sin (that is, to put an end to sin, or to forgive sin).

"To atone for iniquity" is set in a parallelism with "to anoint a most holy place." Here the correlation is obvious. The "most holy place"[165] was that most sacred part of the sanctuary into which the high priest went only once each year on the Day of Kippur (Yom Kippur, the Day of Atonement) to sprinkle the blood of the animal sacrificed for sin on the *kapporeth*, or mercy seat.[166] Thus was expiation or atonement made for sin (see Leviticus 16). In the thinking of the Israelite, the idea of expiation and atonement thus were related to the Sanctuary; more precisely, to the most holy place of the sanctuary.[167]

Gabriel continued: "Know therefore and understand." These two words become hinges which introduce the explanation. Following through on the literary principle of parallelism, the message is articulated in three phases. The three verses containing those phases show perfect symmetry:

A₁ (verse 25a)	B₁ (verse 25b)
From the going forth of the word to restore and build Jerusalem to the Anointed One, a prince seven weeks and sixty-two weeks	Restoration and construction with squares and moat in a troubled time

A₂ (verse 26a)	B₂ (verse 26b)
After the sixty-two weeks the Anointed One will be cut off and and have nothing: no one at His side[168]	People of the prince will destroy city and sanctuary in flood, war and desolation, according to what was cut off

A₃ (verse 27a)	B₃ (verse 27b)
And he shall make a strong covenant with many for one week; and for half (in the midst) of the week he shall cause sacrifice and offering to cease.	Upon the wing of abominations shall come one who makes desolate until the One cut off is poured out on the desolater.

Here again one finds the same diptych (a story from two points of view) effect. In the development of the people theme the figure of a Messiah is distinguishable, while in the wake of the Jerusalem theme the historical destiny of the city appears: the end of the city and the sanctuary.

This paralleling of two themes is not an artificial device. It grows out of the double current that runs through the chapter: people—sin; Jerusalem—sanctuary.

The parallelism is justified, too, by the connection each poetic verse makes with its correspondent by means of common expressions such as this: The three verses on Jerusalem (B) have the Hebrew word *HRC* in common—"cut off " is in B₁ and "decree" (that which is cut off) is in B₂ and B₃.

Likewise, the three verses on the Messiah (A₁, A₂, A₃) refer systematically to periods expressed in weeks. For this reason we have related the sixty-two weeks (A₁) to the Messiah and not to Jerusalem, which is suggested by the Masoretic punctuation.[169] The sentence therefore should be divided after "sixty-two weeks" and not before. Our division follows, moreover, that of the most ancient versions of the Bible, such as the Septuagint and the Peshitta.[170]

The two themes of Messiah and Jerusalem are used alternately, which gives the verses their intertwining configuration:

65

A1 Messiah	B1 Jerusalem
A2 Messiah	B2 Jerusalem
A3 Messiah (implied and understood)[171]	B3 Jerusalem

Lateral parallelism also can be seen between A1 and B1, A2 and B2, A3 and B3:

A1 goes with B1 by the repeated use of the two words "restore" and "construct."

A2 goes with B2 in their common theme on destruction and death.

A3 and B3 are together in their references to temple affairs.

The literary scaffolding here is marvelous indeed. Along with understanding the passage, we have not been able to resist the temptation, despite the risk of undue complexity, to pause and lift the veil and admire the prophet's poetic structure. The prophet's message comes through in the beauty of his poetry, and his literary structure clarifies his objective.

Daniel was tormented by the sins of his people and the destiny of Jerusalem and its sanctuary. So it was that in prayer he interceded with God, on the one hand, to forgive the people's sin and, on the other, to turn His face and look upon the devastated sanctuary. These two phrases are echoed in Gabriel's message, in which he suggests God's answer to Daniel's prayer and formulates the prophecy of the seventy weeks.

The prophecy manifests a dual focus. The first is to finish transgression, to put an end to sin, to atone for iniquity—all this leads to the appearance of a Messiah predestined to be cut off and to cause sacrifice and offering to cease. The second focus is Jerusalem and the sanctuary (with its salvation themes), the construction of both and then their destruction.

The intent of Daniel 9 is for the reader to understand that the Messiah is destined to be a sacrificial victim. The phenomenon of expiation requires the Messiah to be stricken so that the sins of the people might be atoned for.

Yet, beyond theological abstraction, this mystical truth will break into the tortured flesh of humanity (l'Histoire). In order to recognize how and when the Messiah became a reality one must focus on the history of Jerusalem.

The Interpretation in Reality

Two particular points of information are furnished by the prophecy, enabling us to establish the historical facts concerning the coming of the Messiah: (1) a time period of seventy weeks; (2) a date to begin this time period—the decree authorizing the reconstruction of Jerusalem and its temple.

I. *The seventy weeks.* What is to be understood by this expression? Are these literal weeks, or "weeks" to be interpreted by a special key?

Some forty years before, Ezekiel (a prophet who also had been exiled to Babylon about the same time Daniel was) was given a vision in which he witnessed the destruction of Jerusalem *yet to come*. Ezekiel's message, with its theological context (sins of the people), historical context (destruction of Jerusalem), and geographical context (in exile) paralleled Daniel's concern.

In Ezekiel's as in Daniel's time, the divine oracle included the fixing of a definite time period. In Ezekiel's case the time was evaluated in days; and the prophet immediately gave the conversion factor: one day equals one year. See Ezekiel 4:4-7.

That conversion key was obviously known to Daniel. In view of the common subject that concerned both Ezekiel and Daniel, it is most likely that Daniel's seventy seeks (490 days) refers likewise to years. In fact, the continuation of Daniel's words (Daniel 10:3) confirms this. The prophet refers to the three weeks during which he limited himself to a very strict regimen; he makes it clear that he is refering to "weeks of days." Thus, Daniel distinguishes this twenty-one day period from the time period of seventy weeks mentioned earlier, making clear that the seventy weeks were indeed "weeks of years." Daniel's specific reference to "weeks of days" is the only time in the Bible where such words appear.

Furthermore, Jewish tradition has always interpreted the seventy weeks in this way.[172] On the words "seventy weeks [of years] have been decreed [cut off]," the Talmud comments: "This prophecy was given at the beginning of the seventy years of captivity in Babylon. From the restoration to the second destruction, there were 420 years, which makes a total of 490, or seventy weeks of years."[173]

Elsewhere the Talmud is most precise: "A week in Daniel 9 means a week of years."[174]

The Midrash Rabbah follows this same line of interpretation. In explaining the verse "He shall make a strong covenant with many for one week" (Daniel 9:27), he says: "A week represents a period of seven years."[175]

Since then the Jews have remained faithful to this reading; and the most famous of the exegetes, such as Saadia, Raschi, and Ibn Ezra, adopted it unanimously.

Having said the above, if one adopts the Masoretic punctuation ("Until the Messiah seven weeks and sixty-two weeks will be restored. . . . After these sixty-two weeks the Messiah will be cut off"), it is difficult to see how the Messiah appearing after the first seven weeks (forty-nine years) would die sixty-two weeks later, that is, after 434 years.[176]

We have good reason to believe, then, that the break in the sentence structure was intended originally to come *after* the words "sixty-two weeks." In this way the death of the Messiah would follow soon after His appearance, which alone would be plausible. Let us not forget, in the support of this viewpoint, that this punctuation is affirmed by the most ancient versions, such as the Septuagint and the Peshitta, with the Dead Sea Scrolls following suit.[177]

Knowing the nature of this prophetic period, we still must determine the starting point.

II. *The Decree.* "From the going forth of the word to restore and build Jerusalem" Daniel 9:25.

In this connection, the book of Ezra tells us that Jerusalem and its temple were reestablished following a succession of decrees issued by Cyrus, Darius, and Artaxerxes (see Ezra 6:14).

Each one of these kings was to publish a decree relative to the restoration. But that three decrees were necessary, that the first two are insufficient, must highlight the importance of the third. Only the third came to full fruition. Nor does the Bible mention others. The third decree was, in fact, much longer and more substantial in its provisions than the first two. Only the third announces the *total* restoration of Jerusalem.

The decrees of Cyrus (cf. 2 Chronicles 36:22, 23 and Ezra 1:1-4) and Darius (cf. Ezra 6:6-12) concerned only the construction of the temple and its appendages. The decree issued by Artaxerxes (cf. Ezra 7:12-26) provided, in addition to the restoration of the temple, for the setting up of judges and magistrates to administer the civil life of the city (see Ezra 7:24, 25). This decree involved the reconstruction and restoration of the city of Jerusalem—not the temple only. And this third decree was the only one followed by a service of dedication and of praise to God. This service seems to have recognized an answer to prayer, a visitation in which God remembered an ancient prophecy and inspired its fulfillment: "Blessed be the Lord, the God of our fathers, who put such a thing as this into the heart of the king, to beautify the house of the Lord which is in Jerusalem, and who extended to me his steadfast love before the king and his counselors, and before all the king's mighty officers, I took courage, for the hand of the Lord my God was upon me, and I gathered leading men from Israel to go up with me." Ezra 7:27, 28.

Artaxerxes issued this decree in the seventh year of his reign, which was in the autumn of 457 B.C.[178]

Sixty-nine weeks—that is, 483 years later—according to the prophecy, a

Messiah (an Anointed One) prince was to appear. That year would be A.D. 27.

Following the sixty-nine weeks, the Messiah would be "cut off." The remainder of the passage (verse 27) tells us that the Messiah would "cause sacrifice and offering to cease" in the midst of the following week, that is, the seventieth and last of the prophetic period. We already have seen how Daniel, the poet-author, indicated by means of literary parallelism a close relationship between the Messiah and the expiatory ideas expressed in the Levitical system of rites. The violent death (ykaret) of the Messiah[179] accompanies the sudden cessation (yashbit) of the ritual. The two verses relate to the same subject—to the Messiah. He will be cut off, and He will cause the sacrifices and offerings to cease. The two events are inseparable.

Therefore, if the second of the two events takes place in the middle of the week, it must be deducted that the same was true for the first. This leads us to place the execution of the Messiah in the spring of A.D. 31—a half week (three and one half years) after His public appearance (the autumn of 27).

One can understand Flavius Josephus's observation on Daniel: "Everything was extraordinary in this the greatest of the prophets . . . because he did not just predict in a general way that which was to come, as did the other prophets, but he marked the time when it was to take place."[180]

On the same occasion, the historian attests the value of such a book for the Jews of his time[181] (the first century of our era): "Our nation still reads his writings today, and this reading proves how much God revealed Himself to Daniel."[182]

Proofs Abundant

Biblical writings and those of the Jewish tradition convey a strong messianic preoccupation: "All the prophets prophesied only for messianic times," declares the Talmud.[183] The subject of the coming Messiah was of great importance to Jewish thinking, and this rich inheritance is ours to enjoy and study today. We must examine it from all sides in order to understand as best we can its multifaceted meaning.

Many witnesses can be found in Jewish literature to a deep, abiding faith that a personal Messiah was to come, whose redemptive mission would merge in sacrifice. He would save while risking His life. A very Jewish tradition rooted in biblical texts and apparent in the Mosaic rites even dared to see this in its contradictory form: the Messiah would be at the same time God and man.[184]

When preaching concerning this Jeshua of Nazareth broke forth in the cities of Israel, many became followers. Flavius Josephus observed in his book *Jewish Antiquities*: "In that time lived Jesus a wise man. . . . He performed miracles and taught the people who received with joy the truth; and he brought many to go with him."[185]

This response of Jews to Jeshua (Jesus) is easily understood. The traditions, both written and oral, contained teachings that confirmed their new feelings and convictions. From the Levitical rites to the prophecies of Isaiah, everything seemed to announce the coming of a Messiah—God who would save by His sacrificial death. Immediately on His arrival, Jeshua was expressly designated as the "Lamb of God, who takes away the sin of the world." John 1:26.

Furthermore, many people said that they had seen Him perform the most extraordinary miracles. He had even raised the dead to life. Many claimed to have been healed by Him or by His name. Such events were of recent date and could be verified by contemporaries of Josephus. When people of different origin and culture suddenly agreed to tell without the least hesitation and in abundant detail the same story, one was inclined to stop and think. Morever, the conviction of many of these witnesses, whose good faith was tested even to the point of martyrdom, was bound to generate a host of fellow believers. But on top of all this evidence was that bothersome prophecy made by Daniel which claimed to fix the date of the appearance and the execution of the Messiah, respectively, for the years 27 and 31. And this Messiah that came by the name of Jeshua appeared exactly in the year 27: "In the fifteenth year of the reign of Tiberius Caesar." "Jesus, when he began his ministry, was about thirty years of age."[186]

Luke's extreme care in dating with precision the beginning of the Messiah's ministry reveals the importance attached to prophetic chronology. The year of His public presentation demonstrated that the Messiah came when "the time had fully come" Galatians 4:2-4; cf. Mark 1:15. During that period the Jewish world was awash with messianic hopes[187] as though the people were ready to greet and accept the One that was to bring Israel's consolation.

Lastly, no one could overlook that the Messiah known as Jeshua had been executed approximately three and a half years after the beginning of His public ministry,[188] in the year A.D. 31, even as Daniel had predicted.

That Jeshua of Nazareth seemed to correspond in all points to the messianic portrait outlined in the Scriptures became inescapable to a growing number in the Jewish community.

Furthermore, Jewish tradition had retained a messianic conception that strangely resembled that of the gospel. After the separation between Jew and Christian, that is, at the time the tradition was written, Judaism had no desire or inclination to transmit opinions that would be prejudicial to Jewish orthodoxy. The Judeo-Christian controversy was going full blast, and the Talmud and the Midrash were both participants.[189] The fact that these texts we have been considering were nevertheless passed along shows to what degree Israel was immersed in messianic theology; the fact also attests to the honesty of the scribes.

All this argumentation was striking, and it often brought conviction. However, the argumentation was rarely decisive. Remarkably, the gospel record does not give even one case of "conversion" based exclusively on a rational demonstration. In fact, when "conversion" happened, it arose from a different direction, almost contrary to rational argument: acceptance derived from an experience—from personal knowledge. It began with a personal, subjective experience with this particular Messiah and found confirmation in a new reading of the Scriptures.

The case of Saul of Tarsus is a striking illustration. This Pharisee had been trained in the most demanding Jewish schools; he could have concluded, by his own study, that the Jeshua of Nazareth was indeed the awaited Messiah. His thorough knowledge of the Scriptures and of the Jewish tradition were sufficient proofs and ought to have brought him naturally to that conclusion. But they did not. On the contrary, from his erudite, religious approach, he came to the conclusion that the new sect was dangerous; and he set out to destroy its members: "I am a Jew, born at Tarsus in Cilicia, but brought up in this city at the feet of Gamaliel, educated according to the strict manner of the law of our fathers, being zealous for God as you all are this day. I persecuted this Way to the death, binding and delivering to prison both men and women. Acts 22:3, 4.

Only a decisive personal encounter with the One he persecuted led him to reconsider the whole question and to undertake a new interpretation of the Scriptures. Only when armed with this personal experience and backed up by the texts was he able to forge the evidence that Jeshua was indeed the Messiah. See Acts 9:22.

Saul is an example with a meaningful lesson. The Christian religion, resting on the person of the Christ or Messiah, is essentially an experience—a person-to-person relationship. Thus it appears inappropriate to talk about "proofs" when the issue is above all one of life and love. Meaningful encounters with a person cannot be built on mere arguments or proofs. Such encounters, generally unexpected, involve all the faculties of our being: instinctive and rational, mental and physical. Only in what follows the personal encounter—in the daily dialogue—does the reality of a person-to-person relationship find shape and substance; only then does one find proof that such a relationship was a good choice.

Conviction in a person-to-person relationship proceeds from an experience and not the reverse. Hebrew thought, on this point, differs from Cartesian thought. The latter builds experience on thought. "I think; therefore I am." The Bible pictures God taking hold of men and women before they have understood. The mental girding for moral decisions follows an experience: "I am; therefore I think." For the Israelites to know God's answer, they first had to step into the Jordan. See Joshua 3:13. They believed afterward.

Jewish tradition draws the attention of the believer to the fact that, when God addressed Israel to give His law, the people answered: "All that the Lord has spoken we will do, and we will be obedient [Hebrew: "hear" and "obey" are the same word]." Exodus 24:7. Israel's wisdom consisted in placing "do" before "listen." In this they proclaimed the primacy of action over doctrine. The Maharal[190] draws from this text the lesson that obedience to divine laws ought to be elevated above personal conviction.[191] "We cannot arrive at a knowledge of what is true," notes S. R. Hirsh, "without living according to divine laws."[192] The New Testament seems to be in full harmony with this Jewish conception of discovering truth. Reflecting on this theme, Paul describes faith as an action: "Through faith [they] conquered kingdoms, enforced justice, received promises, stopped the mouths of lions, quenched raging fire, escaped the edge of the sword, won strength out of weakness, became mighty in war, put foreign armies to flight." Hebrews 11:33, 34.

"Faith without works is dead," likewise declared James the apostle. James 2:17. Precise, concrete action is set down in the Bible as a first requirement. In other words, one must live with God if one is fully to believe in God. Likewise, one must know the adventure of a personal relationship with the Messiah if one is to recognize Him in the prophecies. A study of the Scriptures brings a ratification of the choice rather than a demonstration of it.

Many Christians are so conditioned from childhood to believe in Jesus that it is difficult for them to conceive of the existence of any other faith. They imagine, somewhat childishly, that they hold in hand absolute proof of the truth. For them the case is settled.

Such Christians run the risk of someday falling into intolerance. Desirous of demonstrating at any price their truth, they end up forgetting that their life alone is the argument par excellence in favor of it.

One should remember the parable attributed to Lessing.[193] A father had three sons. Nearing death, he called them all to his side. "Here are three rings," he said. "One of them has magical qualities, with the power to transform the bearer into a good and wise man. Unhappily, the three rings look identical; and I am not able to tell you which one is the magical one. The son that gets it will demonstrate the fact in his life."

Under such circumstances, to try to test the metal would make no sense. Yet many Christian believers have lost the essence of the biblical message and thus have become lost in endless disputes. Those who have lost the essentials now strive to be right by force. They seek proof in the metal because they are afraid to reveal the real proof in their lives.

The Jew, once he has become acquainted with and has lived the truth of the Messiah, will turn to the Sacred Book to find therein the confirmation and not the basis of his faith. He is then convinced that the Word could never contradict his experience, because the same Spirit inspires them both.

When a Jew accepts the Messiah, he does so because of roots that always have been his. It must never come to his mind that he will have to be uprooted. He remains a branch of the original trunk. Rather than to announce a destruction, Jesus preached a more authentic Jewish piety. Amado Levi-Valensi is right: "One could never say with more vigor than did Jesus, that the Jew is to remain Jew."[194]

Israelite at heart and by faith, the Jew recognized in Jeshua of Nazareth the Messiah of his people—his very own Messiah. The adoption was justified, nourished by a continual reference to his Scriptures and even to his oral tradition. Therefore, to accept the Jeshua did not require conflict with the ancestral faith. The New Covenant was not a break or a separation but, on the contrary, a rebirth of the Everlasting Covenant.

Rebirth of a Covenant

"The great sin of the Christian world, whatever the grandeur of their faith, would be their rejection of the law of God."—Ellen Gould White.
Only Jeremiah in the Old Testament uses the words "a covenant."
Jeremiah 31:31.

A long and tragic story was fast approaching its climax; the prophet was in a state of expectancy, looking longingly toward a new beginning, a new creation. His preoccupation was apparent in his language. Significantly, the word *bereshith* ("in the beginning"), a technical term related to the story of Creation, is not to be found after the book of Jeremiah (see chapters 26:1; 27:1; 49:34). By invoking memories of the Genesis account, the prophet expressed his great desire for a new world. Against this backdrop, Jeremiah developed his theology of a New Covenant.

The apostle Paul quotes this verse (Jeremiah 31:31) to explain what he considered to be the essence of Christianity (see Hebrews 8:9). It seems apparent that Jesus also referred to this text during the last supper. (See Luke 22:20.) Without question, the first Christians used Jeremiah's reference to a New Covenant to establish a definition of what they really were. We now must discover what was understood by this "new covenant." The traditional Christian concept is that a "new covenant" was to abolish the ancient and install a new religious economy. "There was . . . an abrogation of all that constituted the specificity of Judaism," wrote Father Vincent. "That is what Christianity teaches: Jesus Christ abolished the Law."[195]

Same Law

Yet the passage from Jeremiah, which the apostle Paul quotes in full, says just the contrary: "Behold, the days are coming, says the Lord, when I will make a new covenant with the house of Israel and the house of Judah. . . . This is the covenant which I will make with the house of Israel after

74

those days, says the Lord: I will put my law within them, and I will write it upon their hearts; and I will be their God, and they shall be my people." Jeremiah 31:31-33.

The words "I will write it" are, of course, a direct allusion to the Decalogue, the only document that God wrote with His own hand. Verse 32 implied this when referring to the covenant made at Sinai with the fathers after the departure from Egypt. The Law, says God, that I wrote on tables (Exodus 34:1) will henceforth be written in your heart. Then follows the formula that the Old Testament uses systematically to reinforce the covenant and insure its success: "I will be their God, and they shall be my people" (cf. Jeremiah 31:1; 30:22).

The New Covenant that Jeremiah foresees, far from abolishing the old, on the contrary, actually extends it. The imagery suggested by the prophet's language clearly teaches this. The Law until then appeared to the Israelite to be something outside him; now it was to be within—in his heart—to be an integral part of the most intimate secrets of his being. The Law now was to be assimilated, lived, accepted from within; its inner motivating power would supersede outward character of constraint. This experience was to be personal, direct, existential. In this light one can understand what is said in the next verse: "No longer shall each man teach his neighbor and each his brother, saying, 'Know the Lord,' for they shall all know me, from the least of them to the greatest, says the Lord." Jeremiah 31:34.

The New Covenant is a deepening internalizing of the Old.

Jesus also understood it this way. "Do not suppose that I have come to abolish the Law and the prophets; I did not come to abolish [*katalusai*], but to complete [*plērōsai*].[196] I tell you this: so long as heaven and earth endure, not a letter, not a stroke, will disappear from the Law until all that must happen has happened. If any man therefore sets aside even the least of the Law's demands, and teaches others to do the same, he will have the lowest place in the kingdom of Heaven, whereas anyone who keeps the Law and teaches others so will stand high in the kingdom of Heaven. I tell you, unless you show yourselves far better men than the Pharisees and the doctors of the law, you can never enter the kingdom of Heaven." Matthew 5:17-20, N.E.B.

Do not stop at the halfway point in your obedience of God, said Jesus. Do not be satisfied with a legalistic observance. Go much further! And in the verses that follow, Jesus takes up the practical application of this attitude:

"You have learned that our forefathers were told, 'Do not commit murder; anyone who commits murder must be brought to judgment.' But what I tell you is this: Anyone who nurses anger against his brother must be brought to judgment. If he abuses his brother he must answer for it to the court; if he sneers at him he will have to answer for it in the fires of hell [Gehenna]." Matthew 5:21, 22, N.E.B.

"You have learned that they were told, 'Do not commit adultery.' But what I tell you is this: If a man looks on a woman with a lustful eye, he has already committed adultery with her in his heart." Matthew 5:27, 28, N.E.B.

The Law written in people's hearts becomes much more demanding than the Law written in stone. When the Law is internalized, the whole person is involved, including the most intimate motivations—even the subconscious.

In connection with these same verses, the Roman Catholic theologian Tresmontant made this comment: "That which interested Jeshua, was the being in depth, the secrets of the heart. The one who lives this anger, this desire to kill, is a murderer. Jeshua makes his analysis on that level. He places his requirements at that depth. Not only, as the Torah prescribed, thou shalt not kill, but the commandment of Jeshua adds, thou shalt not desire to kill, thou shalt not wish death." Then Tresmontant remarks, "One can see that there was to be no decrease in the requirements as compared to the Torah, but rather an increase."[197]

And there is more. Jeshua's requirements concerned *all* the Law, not just the provisions concerning murder and adultery. His requirements applied to a commandment whose observance was taken for granted at that time: the Sabbath commandment. Then why did this Master who had shown Himself so demanding in His teaching make a sudden turnabout, in expressing certain liberalizing concessions relating to the Sabbath commandment?

He really did not. In his relationship to the Sabbath, as with the other precepts of the Decalogue, Jeshua really asked for a more complete obedience, a more serious compliance.

Because the Sabbath commandment relates to time, it is especially subject to the crafty twists of compromise. A time to celebrate the Sabbath can be adapted to meet changes imposed by differing cultures or by other more particular circumstances. Jesus was well aware of man's cowardice and his inclination to discover the easy pretext.

For this reason Jeshua strongly exhorted His disciples in His apocalyptic discourse: "Pray that your flight may not be in winter or on a sabbath." Matthew 24:20.

One can understand that flight in winter would pose problems of a

76

practical nature because of the rigors of the climate. The fears Jeshua had in mind were fully justified. But "flight on a sabbath day" implied problems of a different nature. Such flight could be critical, involving life or death. Yet Jeshua passed over that real danger, counseling His hearers to pray that their flight would not take place on a sabbath, because that could involve a transgression.

Such religious sensitivity seems surprising at a time such as this, when people would be inclined to look for the easy compromise, the ready-made excuse. Jesus wanted His disciples to avoid a situation in which compromise would appear acceptable and justified.

Jesus also puts us on guard against a superficial observance of the Law. In the New Covenant, the Law cannot be satisfied by mere mechanical obedience, with lifeless gestures; it is concerned with the total human being, including the secret recesses of thought and feeling. Therefore, the observance of the Sabbath will assume in the religion of Jesus a new dimension.

To those who accused Him of having healed a paralytic on a Sabbath day, Jesus gave this in-depth answer: "If on the sabbath a man receives circumcision, so that the law of Moses may not be broken, are you angry with me because on the sabbath I made a man's whole body well? Do not judge by appearances." John 7:23, 24.

One must think his faith. It is not sufficient just to do. It is necessary that action proceed from true conviction. If it does not, Sabbath observance will degenerate into a series of mechanical gestures. The Law is to be in the heart and control the total being. In this, biblical religion is distinguishable from paganism; the gesture holds no intrinsic value in itself. The Old Testament more than once makes this clear: "I will punish all those who are circumcised [in the flesh] but yet uncircumcised [in the heart]." Jeremiah 9:25.

"The sacrifice of the wicked is an abomination to the Lord." Proverbs 15:8; cf. Proverbs 21:3; Isaiah 1:10, 11.

Sacrifices, circumcision, and all other rites instituted by God are useless unless they proceed from heart worship.

Jesus did not detract from the principle in Sabbath rest—far from it. He was determined to clarify its orthodoxy. "Do not judge by appearances." You have the impression that I have violated the Sabbath command. But I do nothing of the kind. Rather, I go farther than you do in order to bring you back to the essential, to the invisible, to the spirit of the Sabbath. One can externally observe the Sabbath and yet violate its spirit. What may appear to be a proper gesture may in fact be opposed to the spirit. Such was the case in John 7. Had Jesus observed the Sabbath formalities expected of Him, He would have violated its spirit and the paralytic would not have been healed.

The revelation at Sinai taught that the Sabbath was a day of holiness, not just a day to stop work. The Sabbath was to be a day when people could renew their relationship with God that may have weakened or broken down during days of labor.

"To do good" (Mark 3:4) on the Sabbath, then, is a normal part of the spiritual program. Jesus occasionally healed the sick on the Sabbath day (cf. John 9:16; Mark 3:1-5; Luke 13:10-17). But in so doing, He in no way intended to abolish the Law. He desired rather to teach that the Sabbath was not merely a gesture of cessation but was a total attitude, a way of being that was responsive to the requirements of sanctification contained in the commandment (cf. Exodus 20:8-10; 31:14; Isaiah 56:2).

The warning Jesus gave against the dangers of compromise and legalism which lie in wait for all believers can only emphasize His requirements for a service in depth: heart worship—a service of love.

One must be careful, therefore, not to judge on the appearances with regard to Jesus and hurriedly conclude that transgression, or even abolition, were involved. When His disciples, in full view on the Sabbath day, picked a few kernels of wheat to satisfy their hunger, Jesus could have taken refuge against His accusers by quoting certain familiar lines in the oral Law: "It is permissible to take with the hand and eat on the sabbath day, but it is not permissible to take with an instrument; such are the words of Rabbi Judah."[198]

If Jesus had quoted Rabbi Judah, the accusations of His detractors would have been nullified. But the Galilean Master was pursuing a loftier objective than that of effective controversy and textual battle. Once again He drew the attention of His listeners to the core of the problem: "The sabbath was made for man, not man for the sabbath." Mark 2:27. Jesus here was not promoting, as C. Tresmontant suggests,[199] a "humanization" or liberalization of the Sabbath. On the contrary, He was underscoring the Sabbath's importance for man's happiness, just as Isaiah had done earlier: "If you turn back your foot from the sabbath, from doing your pleasure on my holy day, and call the sabbath a delight and the holy day of the Lord honorable; if you honor it, not going your own ways, or seeking your own pleasure, or talking idly; then you shall take delight in the Lord." Isaiah 58:13.

If the Law is written in the heart, in harmony with the terms of the New Covenant, one will not observe it unwillingly, as if by outward, painful constraint.

Christianity traditionally has seen in Jesus a reformer bent on abolishing the Jewish Law. But Jesus actually had no thought of casting aside the commandments of God. [200]

Not only was the Law unchanged under the New Covenant, it called for a new spirit—for a profound, authentic obedience—for even greater willingness and happy submission.

Paul understood it this way: "But now we are discharged from the law, dead to that which held us captive, so that we serve not under the old written code but in the new life of the Spirit." Romans 7:6.

The examples of covetousness and adultery chosen by the apostle in Romans 7 (verses 22, 25) show that he was thinking of the Decalogue. He then goes on to explain the importance of that Law and the role it plays in the redemptive process.

Thanks to this Law, man is provided with special discernment regarding good and evil. By contact with the Law, he can know what is good and what is evil and thus can become conscious of his guilt and of the death sentence that hangs over him.

Like a mirror (James 1:23-25) that reflects one's physical characteristics, the Law is able to reflect one's moral characteristics and thus the destiny that awaits lawbreakers.

With this awareness, and beset therefore by legitimate despair, a human being can only then turn to God and ask for mercy. God's answer can be interpreted only as an act of unmerited salvation, a free gift of life.

The Law of itself produces death; but, in another sense, the Law brings life because it forces one to recognize his insufficiency. The Law drives the lost one to cry to God for mercy and grace.

The same thought pattern is to be found at the end of Romans 7. Paul's struggle to live in his human strength according to God's Law ended in total defeat, as he says: "I see in my members another law at war with the law of my mind and making me captive to the law of sin which dwells in my members. Wretched man that I am! Who will deliver me from this body of death?" Romans 7:23, 24.

This stark realization of defeat became salutary because it permitted Paul to recognize his need of the grace of God: "Thanks be to God through Jesus Christ our Lord!" (Romans 7:25). Just like a Greek tutor, a servant assigned the task of taking the pupil to the master teacher, the Law's function is to lead the believer to the Messiah-Saviour. See Galatians 2: 23, 24.

Far from suggesting the abrogation of the Law, Paul demonstrates, on the contrary, the absolute necessity of the Law. For Paul, the Law remains precious and valid: "I delight in the law of God, in my inmost self. . . . So then, I of myself serve the law of God with my mind." Romans 7:22-25.

The apostle believes in a salvation that is freely bestowed. His experience in striving for peace and righteousness on his own convinced him that salvation had to come from outside his feeble efforts. Man cannot save himself. But the good news of the gospel tells the world that God intervenes; He comes down to save mankind. "You are under grace," Paul cries out exultantly. Romans 6:14.

But could not this view of salvation possibly be dangerous? If salvation is a free gift, if it comes from God (Romans 3:24), it must be sure. If my effort is futile and useless, I am free to do as I please!

Not at all. In the preceding chapter, as a sort of precaution Paul anticipates such reasoning in a tight presentation on grace and the Law: "What shall we say then? Are we to continue in sin that grace may abound? By no means!" "What then? Are we to sin because we are not under law but under grace? By no means!" Romans 6:1, 2, 15.

According to Paul, sin, which he equates with disobedience to the Law (Romans 4:15), is much less justifiable within the framework of the New Covenant experience. The difference is that now submission and obedience are by man's converted will and arise from the heart: "But thanks be to God, that you who were once slaves of sin have become obedient from the heart to the standard of teaching to which you were committed." Romans 6:17.

To summarize, Paul's experience was in three phases:

1. The Law given at Sinai in the form of the Ten Commandments can evoke in the heart a feeling of personal failure and weakness, of sin and its condemnation. Eternal death becomes a stark reality.

2. Such awareness is favorable to the development of certain psychological conditions. Only when the human being understands that he is helpless in his own power will he turn in desperation to his God. It is then that salvation appears to him as a free gift, not as something that is due him.

3. This manifestation of God's love, far from becoming a pretext for unfettered disobedience, conveys a divine impulse to obey God. Henceforth one who sees himself as the object of God's love will serve Him in a new spirit—a spirit completely rescued from the tensions of fear and guilt or the desire to earn one's own salvation. Now a peaceful assurance and an unbelievable gratitude prevail.

In other words, obedience to the Law is the expression of our salvation and not the means by which it is attained.

Evidently the apostle Paul applied these three principles in his own life.

Regarding the Sabbath, particularly, we find him observing it regularly, in keeping with the manner outlined in the Law: "Paul as usual introduced himself and for three consecutive sabbaths developed the arguments from scripture for them." Acts 17:2, Jerusalem Bible.

How could he have done otherwise? The Sabbath commandment is an integral part of the Law. In his defense on the Law, Paul does not leave the slightest indication that the Christian religion relaxed the expectations of the Law. The apostle James, in a passage devoted particularly to the Ten Commandments,[201] gives this warning: "Whoever keeps the whole law but fails in one point has become guilty of all of it." James 2:10.

In any case, reasons the same apostle, we are not to "judge the law," for "there is one lawgiver and judge, he who is able to save and to destroy." James 4:11, 12.

Under the New Covenant, the Law remains. Only the attitude of the believer has changed. No longer is he a victim of or a believer in the efficacy of an empty gesture—an externalizing of religion. His service will grow in depth, in keeping with a more intelligent, self-authenticating obedience.

However, this spiritual revolution, this life of repentance, happens only when one grasps in his heart the fact that salvation is a free gift, an act of love, in the person of the Messiah. When one understands that one owes everything to God, then the mentality of a mercenary has been replaced by the mentality of a son, resulting in a psychological difference that all can see. See Romans 8:15-17. The mercenary obeys in order to get something; the son obeys because he already has it. For the mercenary, the Law is eternal, like a government regulation that all must accept; for the son, the Law is within the heart. He serves, not because of a painful obligation, but as a loving response to God's initiative.

Thus the New Covenant brings a deeper, truer obedience. Such obedience, rather than abolishing the Law, establishes it. Exclaimed the apostle Paul: "Do we then overthrow the law by this faith? By no means! On the contrary, we uphold the law." Romans 3:31.

The Two Laws

Yet the New Covenant, by the very nature of the theology of salvation that it implies, does result in the annulment of another category of laws. These laws had one purpose, and that was to announce symbolically the coming of salvation. They were "a type and shadow" of the "substance" (the Messiah) to come. See Colossians 2:17; Hebrews 8:5; 10:1. They were destined, therefore, to disappear with the arrival of the promised Messiah.

The New Testament story makes only one allusion to a time when

81

"shadow" met "substance," and that was in connection with the crucifixion: "And behold, the curtain of the temple was torn in two, from top to bottom." Matthew 27:51.

The meaning of this event was that henceforth access to God was direct, while heretofore God's presence, for the Israelite, was manifest in the most holy place. See Exodus 25:22. Henceforth the Levitical worship, with its system of sacrifices and ceremonial laws, was to be useless and unnecessary.

Had not the prophet Daniel predicted this development? The death of the Messiah was to cause sacrifices and offerings to cease. See Daniel 9:27.

The apostle Paul explains why: "For since the law has but a shadow of good things to come instead of the true form of these realities, it can never, by the same sacrifices which are continually offered year after year, make perfect those who draw near. Otherwise, would they not have ceased to be offered? If the worshipers had once been cleansed, they would no longer have any consciousness of sin. But in these sacrifices there is a reminder of sin year after year. For it is impossible that the blood of bulls and goats should take away sins." Hebrews 10:1-4.

Paul emphasizes the inefficacy of sacrifices that must be renewed unceasingly, because their effect is temporary. His conclusion is clear. The law relating to these sacrifices was to disappear and be replaced by a more far-reaching sacrifice, the effect of which would last forever: "He abolishes the first in order to establish the second. And by that will we have been sanctified through the offering of the body of Jesus Christ once for all." Hebrews 10:9, 10.

The Law that was abolished, then, was the law that related to the sacrifices. Paul says this again in different terms: "by abolishing in his [Christ's] flesh the law of commandments and ordinances." Ephesians 2:15.

Therefore, two very different sets of laws existed in Israel: the ceremonial law, with a transitory, relative character; and the moral law, with an abiding validity, serving as an absolute standard.

Thus, if in the writings of Paul one gathers the impression that at times the law is abolished and, at other times, the Law is maintained, one is not to see a contradiction, but rather the existence of two very distinct laws.[202]

In the Old Testament the Israelite well understood this distinction, since, on God's orders, the Decalogue (Ten Commandments) was to be placed *in* the Ark, while the laws concerning sacrifices were to be placed *alongside* the Ark,[203] suggesting thus a superiority of the first over the second. Also the origin and the giving of these laws revealed a difference:

1. The Decalogue had been written by God (Deuteronomy 10:4), while the ceremonial law was outlined by Moses (Deuteronomy 31:9, 24).

2. The Decalogue was graven on tables of stone—an imperishable material (Deuteronomy 10:3), while the ceremonial law had been written in a book—a perishable material (Deuteronomy 31:24).

3. The Decalogue was entrusted by God to Moses, who himself placed it in the ark (Deuteronomy 10:5), while the ceremonial law was entrusted by Moses to the priests, who, in turn, placed it alongside the ark (Deuteronomy 31:26).

The ceremonial law, temporary and relative, was in contrast with the Law of the Ten Commandments, which was eternal and absolute.

* * *

In spirit, therefore, nothing has changed. The covenant made in ancient times between God and Israel was not canceled in order to make place for a new one. The same people, the same God, the same provisions remain. But the time had come for the set of laws concerning sacrifices and offerings to be superseded by the event they had announced for centuries.

At the same time and by virtue of that event, the relationship between the two partners of the covenant was to be strengthened. On God's level, love became more clearly manifest in free, unconditional salvation. On man's level, worship took on a new dimension: rather than ritual performance, now heart worship.

The Ten Commandments of the ancient Law continued to resound clearly with even deeper requirements. The New Covenant was in no way an evolution. On the contrary, it was a return to the sources, to true repentance.[204] The covenant was to have a new birth; the participants were to find again the love of a betrothal. Cf. Hosea 2:16-21.

In fact, this renewal of the ancient covenant did not offend pious Jews in the first century A.D. Tradition and the Scriptures provided all the elements necessary to adopt the views of Paul the Pharisee without large-scale reservations. The Essenes and the Pharisees had no difficulty admitting the transient nature of ritual law as compared to the moral law. They had been asking for a spiritualization of the sacrificial rites. And they were widely listened to. The only defenders of the Levitical worship were the priests, or the Sadducees, but they were a despised minority and without credibility in Jewish society on matters of religious dogma and authority.

In any case, the future seemed to justify the majority, since, with the destruction of the temple, Judaism was obliged to adapt its worship forms to changed circumstances. For instance, a prayer could correspond to the sacrifice of an animal.[205]

It must be stated clearly: original Christianity never sought, under any pretense, to bring into question traditional Judaism. Whether it was the identity of the Messiah in the person of Jeshua of Nazareth or the conception of the Law as structured in the writings of Paul, everything in the so-called new religion seemed to fit naturally into the mold of tradition.

Claude Tresmontant was right when he lifted his voice against the serious misrepresentation of the facts that Christian circles too often accept and practice: "Often in manuals and elsewhere, Christianity is presented as a softening down of Judaism. Christianity sets itself against Judaism as the religion of charity and forgiveness versus that of rigor and justice. Sometimes Jesus and the God of the New Testament are contrasted with the God of Israel, with Yahweh the God of battle, the God of the Jews. Really this procedure dates from Marcion. The same violent contrast is to be found, though set to a different music, in the writings of Luther. The Lutheran doctrine of the Jewish Law in opposition to 'Christian grace' rests on a misunderstanding of what the Torah really is in Judaism. . . . This opposition between Judaism and Christianity, which has developed since the theoreticians of dualism began their work and continued through the so-called 'de-Judaization of Christianity' by the German theologians and philosophers, is scientifically false on a number of counts."[206]

Jules Isaac, in his outstanding work *Jesus and Israel,* called the attention of believers, whatever their denomination, to the facts: "Nothing could be more vain than to oppose gospel and Judaism—the gospel that Jesus preached in the synagogue and the temple. The truth is that, in consideration of their roots, the gospel and evangelical tradition are closely related to the Jewish tradition."[207]

This we have been demonstrating. As a Jew, one had every reason to accept Jeshua the Messiah and His teaching. The tradition in general led to this. So it was that, by thousands, the Jews listened to the Galilean Rabbi as to One sent from God. However, the drama of the crucifixion did bring a misunderstanding which must be resolved.

The Misunderstanding of the Crucifixion

"We need constantly to exorcize our history."—André Chamson.

The unruly crowd that massed in Jerusalem's praetorium that fateful day and shouted "Let Him be crucified!" was composed chiefly of Jews, was it not? Of course; but before a finger is lifted in scorn to indiscriminately accuse an entire people of a crime, should not the facts be carefully examined? The truth is—the question is not a simple one. The entire story is beset with obscurity and contradictions.

Nothing in the general attitude of the people could have led one to anticipate the reaction of the crowd on that Friday morning. On the contrary, everywhere Jesus went in Palestine, and particularly in Galilee, He met an enthusiastic reception: "Jesus returned in the power of the Spirit into Galilee, and a report concerning him went out through all the surrounding country. And he taught in their synagogues, being glorified by all." Luke 4:14, 15.

"He [Jesus] left there and went to the region of Judea and beyond the Jordan, and crowds gathered to him again; and again, as his custom was, he taught them." Mark 10:1.

"All the people [in Judea] hung upon his words." Luke 19:48.

The crowds that assembled wherever Jesus went generally appreciated Him right up to the end. In the sixth chapter of John's Gospel we are told that "many of his disciples drew back and no longer went about with him." Verse 66. But to conclude from that incident that the people generally were leaving Him would be entirely false. In fact, popular sympathy for Jesus was evident right up to the last, including the final week.

Father Lagrange recognizes this: "Right up to the Passion week, the esteem of the crowd for Jesus never failed."[208]

How is one to explain, then, that sudden hatred for a teacher the people had admired and followed? In His human relationships Jesus was loved by the people. Theologically, He could not have been more orthodox.[209] How then can we reconcile the high esteem the people had for Jesus with the death sentence they did not hesitate to demand at the critical moment?

It could be said, of course, that political opportunism or fickle human changeableness were involved. Crowd instability is also a well-known phenomenon. Yet even taking into account such factors, is it still possible that the throngs that knew Jesus and followed Him with enthusiasm were made up of the same people who ultimately pronounced the death sentence against Him?

However plausible such an interpretation may appear, because simple and direct, it does run counter to logic and the record of events we find in the New Testament. For instance, according to the gospel story, the priests followed every deed and word of Jesus to find some pretext to arrest Him. They knew not how to go at it because "they feared the people" who "hung on his words." Luke 22:2; 19:48. So in order not to provoke a scandal or a tumult (Luke 23:14; cf. Mark 14:2), they decided to bring Jesus to judgment during the night (Matthew 26:31; 27:1), which was a most irregular procedure.[210] The priests did all this with stealth because they were very conscious of Jesus' popularity.

Now, if the priests felt compelled to resort to such subterfuge, it was due to their fear of the people, whose fondness for Jesus was evident and had to be taken into account.

Consequently, those who shouted "Crucify Him!" could not have been, barring a few exceptions, the same people as those feared by the priests.

But who, then, could have made up the throng that crowded into the praetorium?

Who Did the Shouting?

A Minority of Palestinian Jews. To be sure, in the ranks of that motley crowd were some who had known Jesus—some who had been touched by His message. But people forget easily. Often without thought, even unconsciously, they allow themselves to be carried along with the crowd, to the point that events finally take over completely, leading them into unanticipated trouble. Judas, for instance, who betrayed Jesus and turned Him over to the mob, was surprised by the turn of events. He no doubt expected that his Master would react and undo the evil devisings of His enemies by the sheer weight of His power. But this did not take place. Jesus offered no resistance. Then, profoundly disappointed and anxious, Judas said to the chief priests: "He is innocent!" But it was too late to back up. Jesus would be crucified.

Judas did not foresee this eventuality, nor did he want it. What a terrible misunderstanding! How many others, like Judas, clamored for the Messiah's death though they never really wanted it to take place or never understood what was going on! Judas did have an idea in the back of his head: Force the Lord to forego any further dallying and to perform finally as the people expected the promised Messiah to perform. But most of those who shouted were acting with so little conviction that they needed the encouragement of the priests to get into the fray. Contaminated by the evil rumors that had been scattered abroad and carried away by the frenzy of the leaders, individuals lost control of their thinking and their actions. As members now of a crowd, they took up the catchwords that were repeated in hypnotic unison. Reason had fled.

Unconsciously or with cowardice, indifferent or without an opinion, the people who assembled followed the suggestions spoken by the priests; these leaders knew what they were doing and what they wanted.

The Priests. Indeed, the priests led out in this whole matter. They arrested Jesus and incited the people to shout "Crucify him!" Mark 15:11.

According to the apostle John, who was present at the event, the call to "crucify him" came only from the priests. Wrote John: "When the chief priests and the officers saw him, they cried out, 'Crucify him, crucify him!'"[211]

Consequently, when one takes into account the predominant role played by the priests in the crucifixion, one is led to think that the number of Palestinian Jews involved was far from large. The masses knew and loved Jesus. Furthermore, the masses despised the priests, whom they considered to be traitors in the employ of Rome.[212] Flavius Josephus describes the priests as an opulent, rapacious caste, despotic toward the people and servile toward the Romans,[213] who took advantage of their sacerdotal privileges to despoil the religious poor.

That picture of the clergy had made such an imprint on public thinking that the Talmud has recorded a popular song that goes like this: "House of Annas,[214] unlucky me, unlucky me, because of their whisperings! . . . For they are all high priests, and their sons are treasurers, and their sons-in-law are Temple inspectors, and their valets jump on us and thrash us with sticks!"[215]

A Majority of Diaspora Jews. It would seem, therefore, that the crowd massed before the praetorium was made up largely of Jews who not only were unacquainted with Jesus, but who were ignorant regarding the priests and their abuses. The crowd was most probably from abroad. Jesus' reputation had not yet spread beyond the Palestinian frontiers. No Jewish writer of the Diaspora mentions Jesus during that period. Philo of Alexandria, for instance, who was contemporary to Jesus, mentions Pilate but says not a word about the Galilean Teacher.

Remarkably, the crucifixion took place at Passover—a time when many Jews of the Diaspora were in the country. People from the four corners of the earth camped all around Jerusalem. They pressed in close to the city because the Passover lamb could be sacrificed only in the Temple. See Deuteronomy 12:13, 14, 26; 16:2. It must not be forgotten that the Diaspora had been an historical fact for eight centuries and that the majority of the Jewish people no longer lived in Palestine. Perhaps only 7 or 8 percent of the world's Jewish population lived in Palestine at that time.[216]

At the time of the crucifixion, therefore, one could find, in the streets of Jerusalem, Jews from all parts of the world. In other words, Jews that knew Jesus and Jews that had never before heard of Him. The New Testament account alludes to these two categories of Israelites: "When he [Jesus] entered Jerusalem, all the city was stirred, saying, 'Who is this?' And the crowds said, 'This is the prophet Jesus from Nazareth of Galilee.' " Matthew 21:10, 11.

Does this not indicate that two distinct kinds of people mingled in the city at that time? Could it not be that we have here a key to the problem—an explanation of the contradiction we encountered earlier? The crowd that condemned Jesus could have been composed chiefly of Diaspora Jews, who were essentially ignorant concerning both Jesus and the priests. If so, exciting and manipulating their thinking was an easy matter.

* * *

Under the urging of the priests, the clamor broke forth. Perhaps a minority of Palestinian Jews had allowed themselves, by weakness, by lack of forethought and understanding, to be carried along to deny the One they had loved and acclaimed; while the others, perhaps the majority, had followed the same course without really knowing anything about the One they voted to crucify.

Both groups had this in common: they were not exercising the initiative. They had to be incited and inflamed. Their condemnation did not come spontaneously. The crowd had been passive—possibly reluctant. And if this were the case, the people did not sense their personal responsibilities.

Moreover, Jesus understood the situation. He knew how weak men and women were—so easily led and misled. Pleading these extenuating circumstances, and wrenched with pain, He prayed: "Father, forgive them; for they know not what they do." Luke 23:34. Too often this final supplication is forgotten when we recall the fateful words of the throng: "His blood be upon us and upon our children." Matthew 27:25. It remains to be seen which of these two prayers was the most worthy to be heard and answered.

Who Is Responsible?

The Jews. The crowd that the priests had brought together could not really be considered responsible. Misled and incited by the priests, the cooperation of the people was more or less passive. Neither must one forget the presence of the large segment of Diaspora Jews. There are strong reasons to believe that without them the priests never would have been able to achieve their objective. But with them present, the priests were easily able to line up a majority ready to carry out their designs.

All this was easier to do because the only favorable testimony given to the accused was offered by the blood-thirsty Pontius Pilate, whose word had absolutely no credence.[217]

The Christians. The only voices the people would have listened to (because they would have been raised by Jews like themselves) were those of Jesus' disciples, who soon were to be known as Christians. They would have been listened to also because they had something to say. But the New Testament story reports that they remained silent; in fact, most were hiding.

Lazarus who had been resurrected from the dead, John the beloved disciple, and all the others, including many who had been healed or comforted or edified—they knew the truth, but to speak would have been dangerous. When one of them did speak, it was to betray: "Now Peter was sitting outside in the courtyard. And a maid came up to him, and said, 'You also were with Jesus the Galilean.' But he denied it before them all, saying, 'I do not know what you mean.' And when he went out to the porch, another maid saw him, and she said to the bystanders, 'This man was with Jesus of Nazareth.' And again he denied it with an oath, 'I do not know the man.' After a little while the bystanders came up and said to Peter, 'Certainly you are also one of them, for your accent betrays you.' Then he began to invoke a curse on himself and to swear, 'I do not know the man.' And immediately the cock crowed." Matthew 26:69-74.

One can hardly dare imagine what might have happened had the disciples been able to overcome their cowardly fear and had shouted in the face of the multitude the innocence of the just One. Had they only been willing to take sides! Possibly the Diaspora Jews then would have become suspicious of the priestly doings. Who knows but what the priests, facing the threat of a scandal and a riot, might have felt obliged to abandon their deadly scheme?

The Christians knew the stark facts of the situation, but they remained silent. Were they not, in a sense, more guilty than all the others?

Yet, can one really hold this against them? What would we have done in their place? They, too, were overrun by fast-moving events. Confused, they decided to be prudent at all costs.

Be that as it may, their silence, however rationalized, certainly cost the life of Jesus.

The Passersby. Still others must be assigned a part in this fatal guilt: the many Romans and Jews, civilians and soldiers, who passed by that day.

They stopped and looked but did not care enough even to inquire as to what was taking place. Hatched-up accusations? A mistrial? A miscarriage of justice? So what! This cannot be any of our business! Such also took part in the killing of God. Their indifference was just as murderous as the clamor of the multitude. So who can dare sort out the guilt of that tragic day?

A Misunderstanding. Even they who clamored for the death penalty cannot be seriously incriminated. Here we encounted yet another misunderstanding, appearing when a choice is offered between the release of Barabbas and that of Jesus.

Barabbas is the Aramaic equivalent for "son of the father." And if one accepts the content of certain manuscripts that Origen read, the given name of Barabbas was "Jesus."[218] So both were named Jesus! Which of the two was in the mind of individuals in the crowd when, in Aramaic, the release was chosen? There does not seem to be any way to decide this question definitively. To say the least, a doubt beclouds the guilt of those who made this incredible choice.

The Priests. But if guilt there must be, then it seems logical to turn on those at whose hands Jesus said He was to suffer and die. See Mark 8:31, 33; Matthew 16:21; Luke 9:22. On the "rich" whom James accused of putting the "just One" to death.[219] On those who, appointed by the Romans and despised by the Jews of Palestine, could in no way be considered the true representatives of the Jewish people. On those who went contrary to the general feeling of the people and who hid from the people their murderous intention to do away with Jesus. On those who, finally, were jealous of the Master's growing prestige and were alone in having a motive for the crime—that is, on the priests.

Mark records this: "The chief priests and the scribes heard it and sought a way to destroy him; for they feared him, because all the multitude was astonished at his teaching." Mark 11:18.

John wrote, "The chief priests and the Pharisees gathered the council, and said, 'What are we to do? For this man performs many signs. If we let him go on thus, every one will believe in him, and the Romans will come and destroy both our holy place and our nation.' But one of them, Caiaphas, who was high priest that year, said to them, 'You know nothing at all; you do not understand that it is expedient for you that one man should die for the people, and that the whole nation should not perish.' . . . So from that day on they took counsel how to put him to death" (John 11:47-53).

Notice the superb, classical reasoning of the high priest. It was tailored to the occasion and brought the desired result. Caiaphas gave the impression of profound wisdom and a certain generosity at the same time. However, his logic was a glaring monstrosity; it required, in the name of justice and society, the sacrifice in good conscience of the minority for the majority.

But all this cunning in argument must not fool anyone. It remained a cover-up for vile baseness, of which the record says, "He [Pilate] perceived that it was out of envy that the chief priests had delivered him up." Mark 15:10, R.S.V. cf. Matthew 27:18.

The priests alone worked actively to insure the crucifixion of Jesus. The multitude was either passive or ignorant.

The Romans. But one cannot overlook the presence of the Romans. One must not forget that the priests were first of all representatives, not of the people, but paradoxically of Caesar. After all, the Romans carried out the sentence, did they not? True, Pilate washed his hands of the matter in public, but that did not cancel his responsibility. He could have given proof of authority and said No! That power was in his hands.

Even the lowest-ranked soldier of Rome at the scene could hardly claim innocence. The duty to obey does not justify a crime. And war crimes are still crimes—even the worst kind—for they are committed with a clear conscience.

In fact, some historians see in the crucifixion of Jesus capital punishment in the name of Roman obedience. The manner in which Jesus was mishandled, put to death, and buried shows that the case was chiefly of Rome's jurisdiction.[220]

The Gospel of History

The situation focusing on the crucifixion of Jesus was not as simple as it might appear at first sight. Events were historical in nature, which means that they were lived by human beings, that they developed in the midst of contradictions and complexity. It would be ill-advised, therefore, to propose a conclusion which, though seemingly clear, would be schematic and Manichaean, distinguishing the bad Jews from the good Christians and Romans, or vice versa.

Would it not be well, then, to conclude our ridiculous inquest regarding the possible guilt or innocence of all these participants? The crucifixion tragedy involves too many misunderstandings for anyone to be totally absolved.

The jealous priests and the Roman diplomats, both in the same boat, must, of course, be charged with top-priority guilt. But the crowd—Palestinian or of the Diaspora—and early Christians moved in with them: the first by reason of unconscious complicity, the second by reason of cowardly silence. As for the vast majority of those in Jerusalem at that time, then as always, they were *absent*. Many were still asleep when Jesus went on trial. (One must not forget that all this took place during the night; the day was just beginning to dawn when a small crowd was arriving before Pilate.[221] When the masses had awakened, it was already too late. As Daniel-Rops says, "The people were taken by surprise and did not have time to react." All they could do was to attend the proceedings and witness the tragic execution. And because of this, they, too, shared in the responsibility. Ignorance, too, one can say, is sinful. One is not permitted to sleep when the innocent suffer condemnation.

In differing degrees, all of which are hard to measure, no one really can escape this guilt of deicide: Jews, Christians, Romans, priests, high officials and humble citizens, soldiers and civilians, present and absent—all were and are involved in this tragedy.

The historical truth merges here with a more profound, more binding truth of biblical theology and prophecy: "But he was wounded for our transgressions, he was bruised for our iniquities; upon him was the chastisement that made us whole, and with his stripes we are healed. All we like sheep have gone astray; we have turned every one to his own way; and the Lord has laid on him the iniquity of us all." Isaiah 53:5, 6, Jerusalem Bible.

We—all of us—are responsible for the death of Christ.

92

Betrayal and Conversion

"Christians set themselves between the Messiah and the Jews, hiding from the latter the authentic image of the Saviour."—Nicolai Berdyaev.

There was a time when a dialogue was possible. People traveled from place to place and, on the Sabbath, at the gathering in the synagogue, they had much to discuss. The conversation was exciting. The first words of the speaker caught everyone's attention. How well he spoke! The talk concerned a certain Messiah. So the worshipers followed attentively the discourse of the visiting rabbi from Jerusalem. Jew like them, he spoke their language and based his presentation on their well-known scriptural criteria. The Messiah he talked about could be recognized in the texts they read and studied earnestly day after day.

Already it was difficult to be a "Jew." Oppression was hard to bear. Everywhere the Jew was a foreigner. So the Sacred Scriptures had become a welcome comfort. The people held desperately to his consolation. The Scriptures were read and loved and taken to heart.

And the more the rabbi on the platform talked, the more numerous the passages that came to light from the ancient tradition. They were known by heart, and the audience repeated them in unison. Perhaps the speaker was right! Who knows? Perhaps the Messiah *had* come. The traveling rabbi's words were coherent. The stranger exhibited nothing of a pseudo-mystic in search of sensationalism. Well-balanced, serious, knowledgeable, he seemed to know what he was talking about.

So the people turned to the scrolls and to the best-known teachers. The news brought by the stranger seemed plausible. There was meditation and prayer and further verification of the texts. After extended discussion the visiting rabbi was consulted again. Finally, hearts were set on fire by this good news: The One whom the people had awaited, had come! Maran Atha: "The Lord has come."

Life changed and became filled with faith, love, and hope. Life henceforth was centered in Him. Salvation had come—this was now certain. May He soon come back! The people longed for Him. The Aramaic expression, Maran Atha, was also used to express a fervent prayer, Maran-na-tha: "Lord, I pray Thee, come!" Daily life was set to this theme. The expression became a greeting.

The Lord—it was felt and lived—was very near. Christian now that he was, the Jew remained a Jew, for nothing had really changed. The Messiah he had accepted was the One his fathers had proclaimed in word and song. Here was, in fact, an occasion to return across the centuries to a renewal of the Everlasting Covenant. He felt all the better about it that he had reestablished his roots.

When he evoked the person of the One he called Saviour, the Christian Jew thought of a God of life, a God with whom it was good to walk through life, a God who could be loved. This was the God of Israel, the great God Yahweh that he continued to serve.

He came with fellow believers each Sabbath for worship, for an exchange of ideas, for a meal together. The times were indeed happy ones. The people began to dream that this would never end. When one met an old acquaintance at a crossroads, the story was told again and again. Friends listened, were astonished, curious, interested. Sometimes, of course, they were shocked, unhappy, and went on their way mumbling their objections. But never did this posture of communication provoke horror or scandal. The Jew who converted to Christianity had not yet become a traitor.

One day Christianity began to change its face. Its leaders had become inebriated with success. Compromise seemed to enhance the possibilities of more success. Christians became more and more numerous, acceptable, rich, and powerful. Pride became the casual spirit of many. It was then that, with disdain for its roots, Christianity turned outward and sought other roots.

The Church adopted another past, other customs, and observed another law. Everything conceivable was now done to distinguish Christianity from Judaism and to sever any ties with the Jews. A new religion was created as many Christians sought to discard the old. The new had to be different from the old—even opposed to it.

Did the Jews rest on the Sabbath? Sunday was chosen to replace it. An attempt was even made to change the date of Passover (Easter) so that the Christian celebration would not coincide with the Jewish.

Did the Jews worship a powerful, just, and almighty God? The effeminate figure of a wax-doll Jesus will be created. And justice and righteousness were replaced by "love." This love was not to be the authentic type that flows from the depths of the heart, virile and frank; rather this was to be a roguish, finicky, ofttimes hypocritical love—a love that wanted to be love without speaking straight. This came to be known as so-called "Christian charity."

Did the Jews believe in a living, invisible God? Soon, well-cut statues of a God in perpetual agony would appear everywhere. And the religion of life known to Israel was replaced by a religion of death. The joyous feast days of ancient times marked by laughter and enthusiasm soon were to be replaced by sinister ceremonies symbolized by an instrument of death and torture.

An entirely new mentality appeared—one of mourning, mortification, and taboos. A new civilization came into being in which the Jew was to be a stranger, belonging to a different race. Suddenly, Jesus was no longer a Jew! He was created a blond with blue eyes. Zeal went so far as to try to demonstrate "scientifically" His non-Jewish origin. Christianity, it was said, owed nothing to Judaism. As for the Old Testament, it was relegated to the category of ancient, irrelevant documents without credibility.

With the passing of time, the fissure became a chasm. Everything seemed to cast the new religion into a total opposition to the old. The new had to be in every case whatever the old religion was not. The inevitable arrived. Contempt was born in the heart of the Jew for all that the new religion came to be.

A feeling of hatred on both sides became almost commonplace. Reasons were advanced for this attitude. For instance, the Jews were now accused of the most terrible of crimes.[222] They were said to be guilty of having executed God! Soon the Jews were cursed, then hunted, then confined to their own quarters, then gassed. And all this was done with a clear conscience: *"Gott mit uns* [God with us]."

After all that, to ask a Jew today to be converted to Christianity really means to ask him to deny his identity, to betray his own people and his God.

In the beginning, the situation was very different. When Paul addressed his fellow religionists, he could expect some success. The Jews listened to him, and many of them were baptized. This rite, which was practiced currently in Judaism at that time, did not at all imply a renunciation of Jewish origins and the adoption of a new religion. It implied, rather, a desire for cleansing and a decision to live a life more fully dedicated to the God of Israel. Conversion was a rebirth of the everlasting covenant with that God. Conversion was not at all an uprooting; it was, on the contrary, a confirmation of roots. By becoming a Christian, one became more truly a Jew.

But times changed. Christianity rid itself of everything that might recall its Jewish origins; in so doing, it lost its true identity.

In fact, whenever Christianity undertakes to exorcize everything Jewish about its origins and its doctrine, the danger must be seen that the flower of Israel, Jesus Christ Himself, will also disappear. But what is Christianity without the Christ?

The Jew has been tragically short-changed in this development. While Christianity has withdrawn from him, even setting itself up in opposition to him, Judaism has gone off in the opposite direction. By reaction, everything has been eliminated from its own genius that might suggest an affinity with the Church.

Do Christians read the Bible? Then the Jew will emphasize the tradition—its Talmud.

Do Christians invoke the name of Jesus of Nazareth? Then let the Jew say nothing about Him. Even to pronounce His name would be blasphemy! Nor did it ever come to mind that it might be well to consult the sources and find out exactly what was involved. The matter had been settled in advance: this could not be the Messiah. Why not? The proof was very simple: Jesus of Nazareth was the Messiah of the Christians!

And to make the case complete, the Scriptures, the tradition, were to be read with a different interpretation. Did the Christians propose a personal Messiah? Then an effort will be made to build a framework of Messianism based on a corporate Israel. This brand of theology has even influenced translations of the Bible. [223]

Did the Christians show disdain for the Jews? In reply there would be talk about the goyim. Was it made shameful to be a Jew in Christian society? Then let it be a disgrace for a converted Jew to admit conversion even to his closest friends. When he was present, heads were shaken in disgust. He was excommunicated from Jewish society.

It is no exaggeration to say that the Jews since Christian times have forged a good part of their theology, culture, and mentality in conscious opposition to Christianity. One might even wonder if they now do not owe their very identity to that age-long clash. Sartre must have felt this was true when he wrote that "anti-Semintism created the present-day Jew." [224]

Hemmed in by suffering and humiliation, the Jew has cast himself in the role of a reactor. This became his state of being, though little has he realized to what extent he thereby has risked the loss of liberty and his own real identity.

The entire development is a vicious circle, from which, as a clear analysis must show, there is no way out. Christianity broke from Judaism, and in so doing renounced its natural roots and implanted itself elsewhere. Reacting to this, Judaism has indulged in a long leap that has carried it beyond its natural habitat. In so doing, Judaism has lost some of its original self, approaching even the line of partially betraying its own integrity. The more Christians became independent, the more determined was the Jew to refuse any form of dialogue; in fact, he became more and more aloof.

The Jews did not refuse to accept Jeshua the Messiah simply because they were stiff-necked or pharisaical, nor were they insensitive to His message. The history of Christian origins tells us, on the contrary, that the first Christians were no doubt all Jews; and there were many of them. The writings of the Jewish tradition reveal, furthermore, a considerable natural inclination toward the Christian message. The rabbis of the period were not far from the idea of a Messiah as understood in the gospel story. But a rupture came. Christianity, which originally had its roots in Israel, adopted another law and became the enemy—the persecutor. All this made it virtually impossible for the Jew to embrace the Christian faith.

Thus one can say that Christianity's betrayal created an obstacle to Jewish conversion. Martin Luther, of the sixteenth-century Reformation, understood this very well: "Had I been a Jew," he said in rather crude language, "I would have preferred to become a pig rather than a Christian, considering how those blockheads and jackasses govern and teach the Christian faith."[225]

It would seem, then, that in order for the Jew to be converted without betrayal, the Christian will have to be converted, both in his mental presuppositions, and his theological system. As a result, Israel will be able to undertake a new reading of the Scriptures and the tradition without that age-long, built-in hostility. Only then will the Jew feel free and uninhibited. Who can say that this new tack will not open new paths? This dream has been envisioned by Amado Levi-Valensi: "Could it be, in this time of councils, when the modern Church has undertaken to lighten its dogmas making them more acceptable, that somehow, rethinking its foundations, something nearer apostolic Judaism will come forth? If so, we will find again and together the paths of Revelation and of History.[226]

Such a dream seems almost a fantasy.

Both Christianity and Judaism find it hard to back up, so accustomed are they to their contradictory postures. The worst fear is that, in this mood of reciprocal rejection, both might lose sight of their true identity. Both are old and tired and wrinkled in form and thought. Can they ever expect to break forth in the virility and strength of youthfulness?

It is indeed late. One can hardly expect to redo history and remake peoples. Yet, in an atmosphere of transparent honesty, one must attempt a breakthrough. Alone with one's God, liberated from every outside influence and reaction, one must undertake the great quest for a true source. That source will be found far from today's civilization, far from all forms of intellectual and spiritual contamination, well separated from jostling humanity. Perhaps such a source will reflect to us at long last the true face of our faith and its original purity.

Drinking at the Sources

Today more than ever we have need of a norm centered outside ourselves. Pressed from all sides, people are bewildered, hardly knowing to what saint to pray—if any!

Charlatans and quacks abound, while age-old superstitions, paradoxically, are gaining ground among so-called advanced and open-minded people. Psychics in growing numbers offer their services to a credulous, unsuspecting public.

New religions appear regularly in the religious marketplace, all claiming to possess the one and only "truth."

From time to time waves of religious emotionalism grip public thinking, but soon subside as a passing mood. The so-called charismatic movements make their appeal in the name of Jesus. They are packaged attractively and are received with substantial sympathy. One must wonder, nevertheless, to what extent they are simply the romantic expression of a pent-up sentimentalism.

Some self-styled Christ occasionally appears, claiming to be a reincarnation of Jesus of Nazareth. All of them proclaim, of course, with endless arguments and fire in their voices, that they alone are God's true messengers.

On the other hand, certain humanistic philosophies are set forth, such as socialism, Marxism, and existentialism. Here, they say, at long last, is found the key to happiness and the solution to our problems.

The last few decades have thus witnessed a full-blown array of ideas and religions inspired by the human desire to worship and to find religious authority. This could be the explanation for the current fancy for Buddhism and Oriental mystics, in which man usurps the place of God, both in nature and destiny. Even the famous theories of organic evolution, not excluding the poetical musings of one like Teilhard de Chardin, owe their impulse to that consuming passion. Everything, it would seem, must emerge from below—must arise from within man—and God is no exception!

It is not astonishing, then, that truth today can charm so many pretenders for her hand, and that so much confusion troubles people's minds.

To be sure, goodwill is not lacking. Never have so many colloquiums and round-table discussions been organized in an effort to communicate, to bring reconciliation, to attempt an impossible ecumenism. But the confused buzzing of all this chatter has tended to smother even further the true Word. Today's civilization talks too much, and that is why very little is said.

Very little of importance is said, because God is no longer allowed to speak. Nothing really is said, because civilization claims to be the sole spokesman. The thoughts of men have taken the place of the truth of God. The result: noise, words, confusion. This is the cause of the uneasiness and anxiety that fill the world. Kierkegaard observed, "The world in its present state—our total life—is sickness. If I were a physician and were asked for counsel, I would answer: Be silent, stop talking; otherwise the word of God can never be heard. Even though one might shout noisily and with sufficient strength to be heard in the midst of such tumult, what would be heard is still not the word of God."[227]

Because man has made himself the grand initiator of truth, our society has given birth to a vast marketplace where everyone extols his merchandise and no one hears. As for the potential clients, many end up fleeing from the confusion in something bordering on a state of shock. They have tasted one source after another; and, anxious and undecided, they stagger away in their incoherence.

Others are stronger and more choosy. After all, the spectrum of choice is large. So these industrious souls, like intellectual gourmets, take a little here and a little more from over there, determined to create for themselves a personal religion—a philosophy of their own. They think thus to dissipate the haunting complexity of their life. They run no risk to be mistaken, because everyone is right! Too bad if the system lacks coherence and makes no real sense!

But what about that vast concourse of people who, without spiritual preoccupations, think only of material success, amusement, and food? Such have set up a life-style in their ignorance; they have lost the truly human outlook.

More than ever before, people need something bigger than themselves;

they must have the Word from above which can shed light on their perpetual fumbling and groping here below. History teaches us that when man sees himself as the source of truth and belief, the result invariably is pride and intolerance, if not disarray and confusion. Moreover, Judaism and Christianity have not been entirely sheltered from these dangers, though both were based on a revelation from above. The reason: the human voice, even in Judaism and Christianity, became predominant.

Both Jew and Christian took pride in their understanding of truth, as though each was its author and exclusive depositary. Finally, each one despised and condemned the other with an unalterable anathema, "You are a stiff-necked heretic!" Hardly ever after the rupture in the fourth century A.D. was either ready to engage in meaningful dialogue. Both went more or less into a spiritual ghetto. What was first a message of love and justice became a pretext for hatred. The sweet water of the source became mixed with bitterness. Having tasted both waters, one cannot but thirst after the truths of ancient days—a source without pollution. This would be rainwater from above—"a spring or a cistern holding water shall be clean." Leviticus 11:36.

Bitter Water

"Many men died of the water, because it was made bitter." Revelation 8:11. Here one must not become indulgent and overly sensitive. To denounce imminent danger is to forewarn and to prevent death. This bitter water, which, in Jewish and Christian circles, is self-satisfaction tainted with intolerance and racism, must be eliminated at all costs. To this point Jules Isaac declared: "The anti-Semitism of Christians and the anti-Christianity of Jews are equally an insult to God."[228]

One must not run, then, the risk of missing the point by the use of diplomatic, vague words. With a view to edifying and to getting results, one must be categorically clear.

Of course, a presentation such as this cannot hope to be exhaustive. Only a starting point can be indicated, from which the reader can go on to a personal judgment.

The Duty of the Christian. First of all, the honest Christian is duty-bound to recognize the existence and the horror of anti-Semitism and to measure the weight of its dire consequences.

Let him not be hasty to accuse others; rather, let him look at himself carefully to see if, perchance, the faults he thinks to see in the Jews are not also in him! Psychologically speaking, one often is quick to make a personal scapegoat of a Jew. The psychiatrist Baruk pointed out that some want to "heap on him their hatred—even the worst of hatreds, the one in which they mask self-hatred."[229]

The Christian must be sure, too, not to mask the nature of his feelings toward Israel after all, when they take on a political hue. It is not fashionable today, after Auschwitz, to be anti-Semitic.

Basically, the Christian must begin with a goodwill effort. Admission of a personal and historical problem is halfway to success.

Language and vocabulary need to be changed, for language exercises a strong influence on thought. The prophets in Israel recognized this by urging the people to include or not include certain words in their speech.[230] To be more precise, the Christian should adopt a new language in which the word *Jew* is not automatically synonymous with usury, avarice, double dealing, and business cunning. Let him refrain from all generalizations, such as "the Jews are like that," "that is typically Jewish," "what else would you expect from a Jew," or, paradoxically, "I love the Jews." These and similar expressions reveal prejudice.

The Christian must dedicate himself to this personal revolution—to this linguistic purification. These apparently innocent words imply, consciously or unconsciously, the poison of anti-Semitism. Without exaggeration, these simple words are proof that the Christian has not yet resolved within himself the problem we are talking about.

But there is a greater reason for abandoning these expressions: they simply are not true! The reality is different, and such expressions are nothing less than slanderous. Their use blocks any possibility of communication between the Jew and the Christian.

It will not suffice, of course, merely to abstain from using such words in the presence of Jews. One must learn self-control in their absence! The goal is not just to please the Jews, but to insure one's own well being. Anti-Semitism is a disease of the mind. By curing oneself of it one achieves a certain mental purity and finds at last a better balance in life. Even a certain control of the subconscious is essential to this detoxification.

This personal revolution goes beyond mere expressions; it concerns the thought process. The Christian will want to shed all his prejudices. At the very first indication of a suspicious reaction, he will say to himself: "That is false!" And he will chase the thought far from him—his reason, his understanding, his knowledge will lead him to do this.

The Christian will not remain barricaded, on this question, in an obscurantism worthy of the Dark Ages. He will read and study the Old Testament and the Jewish tradition. His preconceived ideas will disappear automatically, and he thereby will better understand his God and the gospel. Let the Christian exercise care over educational systems and teaching. Here especially he will engage in a task fully worthy of his faith. By exorcizing the demon of discrimination and intolerance that might be lodged within the heart of the child, he is fulfilling a divine trust. He no longer will linger with complicity in a misunderstanding of scriptural passages that seemed to justify his prejudices. So often, personal defects rest on a false reading of Scripture. Thus the Word of God is re-created in the reader's own image. This is a fatal and dangerous practice. The shadows cast by such interpretations outline the fires of death at the persecutor's stake.

Christians must recognize once and for all, as did Vatican II, that it is "a theological, historical, and juridical error to hold the Jewish people responsible for the suffering and death of Jesus Christ."[231]

And after all, is it not nonsense and contradictory to call oneself a Christian while nurturing—consciously or unconsciously—anti-Semitic sentiments? Face-to-face with every Christian stand Jesus, Mary His mother, His disciples, and the Bible—and all were Jewish. In fact, "salvation is from the Jews." John 4:22.

The Duty of the Jew. Two dangers lie in wait for the Jew.

Tormented by anti-Semitism, the Jew can be tempted to engage in self-destruction.[232] But he must not renounce his essential nature, his original roots. Neither should he find it necessary to seek assimilation, even conversion, in order to merge with the majority to achieve success.

Nor must the Jew hide his origin, as one would an unsightly blemish. To do so would provide some justification for the anti-Semite. The Jew's duty, among others, is to make himself see clearly his own mistakes—frankly, systematically, but without ever conceding to a compromise or to silence.

The Jew must be careful not to consider himself to be what the legend has made him out to be: cunning, dishonest, and a lover of money. Let him understand that there is no such thing as a Jewish race, and that there is therefore no other reason for him to believe himself inferior or superior "biologically" to others. It would be perverse for the Jew to transform into truth the prejudices of the civilization that surrounds him.

On the other hand, deliberately to join his persecutors in perpetuating hatred and disdain is to opt for the easy exit, to hide a frustrating complex, and, in any case, to be lacking in objectivity.

When the Jew refuses to be ashamed of being a Jew and is no longer content to remain ignorant regarding his own culture, only then will he fully appreciate its value and particular genius; only then will he be proud of being a Jew.

The aggressions of which the Jew daily is a victim, the horrible history to which he is constantly mindful, can provoke disproportionate reaction. The Jew tends to overreact,[233] falling into the opposite extreme of rejecting nervously and systematically everything that approaches him from the other side.

The Jew should never become aggressive toward the Christian who begins a discussion with him. He must cease to discover anti-Semitism on every hand. To be sure, the phenomenon is so frequent that Jews, who really are the only ones to see and experience it, are tempted to believe in its omnipresence. But such an attitude exasperates the Christian of good will and discourages dialogue.

The Jew must find tolerance in his heart for the Christian—even for the converted Jew. We are thinking especially of the convert's situation in a Jewish milieu, in Israel. The Jew must not allow himself to fall into the same misconceptions that have caused his own torture for centuries. Having put aside all intolerance, he must admit that another Jew may think differently than he, even so far as to believe in Jesus. The Christian Jew must still be considered a full brother, worthy of esteem, even though his conversion may be hard to understand. The Jew will be further obligated to guard himself from any disrespect for Christian culture and truth when they are sound and just. In fact, the Jew should become informed by reading and objectively studying the New Testament as another fruit of Israel's genius, which it is.

The Jew must not allow himself to be carried off by blind reaction; rather the wise do well to take advantage of values wherever found, despite any distaste that might be inspired by the truth-bearer.

Without question, the task is far from easy; indeed, it must be considered beyond human strength. It consists in responding to hatred with love, to scorn with attentiveness. So the great Hillel taught: "The man of strength is he who makes his enemy into a friend."

In Search of a Dialogue

When one becomes aware of all the obstacles, one is tempted to settle for pessimism or for a superficial, noncommittal encounter. And this is why we must now stake out a path toward authentic dialogue.[234]

Liberty. The Jew and the Christian who make a decision to start on this difficult path must refrain totally from passing judgment on the other, from enclosing one or the other within biological, psychological, or theological definitions and labels. Each must enjoy perfect liberty. To box up another in rigid formulations, expressed or not, is to compromise in advance any possibility of understanding. The Christian should forget that he is involved with a Jew, and conversely; otherwise each will feel compelled to play a role, to defend his group position, in which case the idea of dialogue and honest inquiry will be warped at the outset.

The Risk. However well-intentioned the partners to dialogue may be, the encounter can end in failure when both are content simply to present two different points of view—when each brings with him his own program, his particular truth. If at the end of the discussions both have remained essentially on their original positions, if nothing has changed in them to turn them around and cause them concern for previously held positions, proof there is that the dialogue has not even started. Both must be ready to accept a risk—the risk of understanding on deeper levels, and possibly making a mistake. Both must believe that each has something important to learn from the other, something that might bring into question the thought systems and destinies involved. The dialogue table must be approached to learn rather than to teach.

He who pretends to be rich and in need of nothing is condemned in prophetic terms to be "wretched, pitiable, poor, blind, and naked." Revelation 3:17.

Dialogue is not compromise, either. It does not mean mutual agreement in order to be cordial and agreeable or to compensate, so to speak, for bitter altercations in the past. Both must, while remaining open-minded, stand firm for the right without easily bending for reasons other than truth.

A Common Norm. Finally, there should be adopted a "common value" to which both can refer throughout the discussion. Albert Camus poses this principle as a sine qua non of all human reconciliation. Writes Camus: "If men cannot refer to a common value recognized by all in each one, then man is incomprehensible to man."[235]

For our purposes, that norm would be spiritual in character, implying the element of divine revelation. Is not the purpose of the vertical relationship to make more effective this horizontal relationship?

On the basis of this path, which we scarcely have outlined, one can look forward with excitement and hope. Victory will be difficult and perhaps infrequent; but the effort will be worthwhile, as Martin Buber writes: "I become through my relation to the Thou; as I become I, I say Thou. All real living is meeting."[236] In this area of Judeo-Christian reconciliation, the terrain is virtually virgin territory, awaiting exploration. This is nothing short of a challenge to history, a wager on man and on the power of God, a message addressed to our sense of responsibility.

Mixed Waters

"What do you gain by going to Egypt, to drink the waters of the Nile? Or what do you gain by going to Assyria, to drink the waters of the Euphrates?"
Jeremiah 2:18.

It is very simple to take a forthright position regarding the empoisoned beverage known as racism (in all its forms). But to determine one's attitude on that amazing and tortuous stream the centuries have come to call "tradition" is another matter.

Yet tradition gives character and grace to the countryside. To tradition we owe the genius of *cultures*. To ignore tradition is to sacrifice some very essential values.

Indeed, the study of tradition reveals profound wisdom and genuine piety. It must be consulted if we are to understand revealed truth with its historical and prophetic implications.

At the same time, however, one can rightly question, taking into account tradition's origins (not a revelation), whether in the course of history these floodwaters may have broken up into smaller, disconnected streams that now flow only because of the original impetus. Since tradition's mission was to enhance and explain an ancient message, one does well to remain conscious of the risks inherent in any tradition.

The basic risk is that in a desire to adapt to changing circumstances, new concepts may be incorporated into the body of belief, capable of altering or even contradicting the original ideas. Thus the question arises regarding the authority of tradition and the nature of its inspiration.

Tradition by Itself

The rabbis, like the Church fathers, have referred to a double tradition: written and oral, both complementing each other.

In the introduction, the Mishna defines oral tradition as "an enclosure planted around the Torah."[237] This walled enclosure was first a pre-cautionary measure. Were one to get too close without rightly understanding the Law (Torah), one could be led inadvertently to commit a transgression.

Eventually the Mishna served as a way to adapt precepts to particular circumstances, implying thus a "continuous evolution." The Talmudist Rabbi David Malki underscored the need of such an approach: "This permits us never to remain behind the evolution of real-life situations, and to be able to put forth a permanent effort aimed at maintaining equitably those essential qualities of the Torathaim: life-realities, a link with history, current events, 'modernity.'"[238]

Oral tradition is above all a work-instrument—a precaution designed to safeguard the integrity of the divine commandments. The tradition is not the commandment but is subject to it. The image used in this connection by men of wisdom is very suggestive: Oral tradition is to tradition what the walled enclosure is to the field.

One can find the same idea in Christian theology. Facing the Protestant Reformation, which had brought into question the prerogatives of the Church by the enunciation of the principle *sola scriptura,* the Church came forward with the idea of "Scripture and unwritten tradition." A Roman Catholic Bible Dictionary states: "It is essential to ecclesiastical tradition [oral] that an evolution within contingent forms take place in order to conserve the apostolic trust by adapting its presentation to the times and the mentalities to which it is transmitted."[239]

There one also has to deal with two traditions—the one in a fixed, unchanging form; the other more pliant and evolutionary, making possible an "intelligent" transmission of the first. Oral tradition is thus a means to serve the written tradition. The Church recognizes a like view in the words of the authoritative *Encyclopedia of Faith:* "The two traditions are not identical. Between them are decisive differences. Apostolic tradition is a divine thing. There the apostles are organs of the Holy Spirit. God Himself delivered to them the message of salvation in Jesus Christ. Ecclesiastical Tradition is, on the contrary, a human process."[240]

Oral tradition, both in Judaism and in Christianity, is essentially human activity. In any case, it is thus that it defines itself in both systems. A prophetic pretention is never invoked by either one for oral tradition. The rabbi and the Church father do the work of a commentator but not of a prophet. They transmit an opinion—that of the masters, of their ancestors, of their school of thought, or of their time or even themselves—but never an unqualified message from God.

Tradition certainly deserves our respect and attention; but to what extent can it be considered a norm of reference, since it recongizes itself to be essentially of human inspiration?

A Normative Example

Although internal study of tradition would be very revealing as to its relative value, such a study would go beyond the framework of this book. It must be noted, however, that many times the opinions professed within tradition not only betray their foreign source, but show themselves to be in flagrant contradiction with the teachings of revelation. Such is the case, for instance, with the idea of the immortality of the soul. This concept is never expressed in the Bible. On the contrary, the Old and New Testament indicate clearly that after death there is nothing until the resurrection and that immortality is exclusively an attribute of God.

"The living know that they will die, but the dead know nothing, and they have no more reward; but the memory of them is lost. Their love and their hate and their envy have already perished, and they have no more for ever any share in all that is done under the sun. . . . Whatever your hand finds to do, do it with your might; for there is no work or thought or knowledge or wisdom in Sheol, to which you are going." Ecclesiastes 9:5-10.

"The dead do not praise the Lord, nor do any that go down into silence." Psalm 115:17. "The . . . Lord of lords . . . alone has immortality." 1 Timothy 6:15, 16.

A large number of theologians, both Jewish and Christian, recognize this biblical fact.[241] Rabbi Michel A. Weil writes in his book *Judaism: Its Dogmas and Its Mission:* "Let us admit that it is an illusion to expect to find in the Scriptures a direct, clear, or precise enunciation of such immortality."[242]

The Christian theologian R. de Pury is just as categorical: "The Bible, on which must be based our preaching, has nowhere the smallest trace of a belief in the immortality of the soul."[243]

How is it, then, that this idea came to exist in most Bible-based religions?

For the *Jewish Encyclopedia* there is no doubt: "Belief in the immortality of the soul came to the Jews after their contact with Greek thought, particularly through Plato's philosophy, its principal representative."[244]

The Christian theologian André Lamorte echoes this same opinion. Denying the biblical origin of this doctrine, he calls the concept of the immortality of the soul "a pagan idea and more exactly Platonian."[245]

A new belief was thus added to the creed of many religions. Do we find here simply the development of an idea already grounded in the revealed Word? Certainly not. Not only is the idea of immortality of the soul foreign to the Bible, it is entirely incompatible with the biblical teaching on the resurrection. What, indeed, could it serve to believe in the resurrection, if in any case the soul is immortal?

Oscar Cullmann, a Christian theologian, was right to say, "Our answer to the question of immortality of the soul or resurrection of the dead in the New Testament, will be clear. This doctrine of the great Socrates and the great Plato is incompatible with the teaching of the New Testament."[246]

And one can understand that Josué Yehouda, initiator of the movement for unity within Judaism, refuses to conceive of immortality separated from the resurrection: "When the idea of immortality penetrated Judaism, it only meant the resurrection of dead bodies from the dust at the last judgment. Even this idea of resurrection did not separate the soul from the body. That separation is, on the contrary, a classical belief in the Greco-Roman tradition and in that of the Hindus."[247]

Tradition, then, has brought us to an impasse where we must take a position. A compromise is not possible. Either one accepts the Bible and its faith in the resurrection, or one recognizes the authority of tradition and admits the thesis that claims immortality for the soul. A choice is necessary.

There are numerous examples of contradictions between the Bible and tradition. Many contradictions exist even with the tradition. One rabbi professes to believe that the dead are unconscious.[248] Another believes in native immortality. And the Talmud even records discussions on this subject between doctors with differing opinions.[249]

Likewise, Christian tradition engages in a sharp controversy on the subject.[250] A church leader like Justin Martyr does not hesitate to say that any Christian believing in the immortality of the soul is guilty of heresy: "If then you encounter people who call themselves Christians," says he, "who deny the resurrection of the dead and claim that at death their souls are taken to heaven, do not consider them to be Christians."[251]

"A house divided against itself can not survive." Let each one decide, then, for himself.

The Lessons

The real values of the tradition must not lead us to forget that, after all, they are a human process, whose direction is humanly oriented. However great may be the authority and the wisdom of the human agent that transmits it—the Synagogue or the Church—tradition cannot and must not claim the same inspiration as the sacred Scriptures.

To be sure, one owes to tradition the adoption of the canon. So one is greatly tempted to attribute to tradition a special power: it "can bind and unbind." But the fact that such a responsibility was given in the providence of God does not mean that tradition is to be the supreme arbiter above the Bible. By indicating the limits placed on this sacred trust, tradition recognized its own judge[252] and placed itself strictly under the authority of the Bible. Because a slave decided freely to serve a certain master, that power to decide does not make him his master. It would never come to the mind of the slave to place in doubt or to contradict the words of his lord under the pretext that he chose the lord. Because of his choice, his submission will be all the more perfect. The fact that tradition determined the canon is a further reason for it to be subjected to that canon.

Therefore, when one takes into account, as one must, the nature of tradition, one must place it in such a way that it may be critically examined under the strong lights of Holy Scripture.

Tradition remains a fertile field of study, permitting us to better understand the facts of revelation; but if tradition is to play its role properly, it must be looked at as a working instrument to be consulted but never a replacement for the prophetic Word.

Let it be noted, too, that it is tradition, whose genius is chiefly cultural, that has thwarted all attempts at dialogue between Judaism and Christianity. Both have failed to recognize that the one value common to both—the truth that comes from above—should always and consistently remain their common normative authority.

Rain From Above

"The land which you are going over to possess is a land of hills and valleys, which drinks water by the rain from heaven. . . . And if you will obey my commandments . . . to love the Lord your God, . . . he will give the rain for your land in its season." Deuteronomy 11:11-13.

God is no longer in style today. Man insists on having *his* say. On every side one can see the influence of Marxist and existentialist thinking. Though often an unconscious impact, it is there; and it has led this generation to construct a man-centered plan of salvation. Such is the hard core of today's revolution. Even Christianity, in fact, has become a well-muscled political force set on establishing here below the kingdom which formerly was expected to descend from above.

Judaism has likewise opted to march to this music. In Israel, for instance, the battle for survival and the consuming necessity to build homes and to provide life's sustenance are so urgent that there is no time and little desire to think about what has come to be thought of as "myths" from former days of oppression.

In Israel, as elsewhere, a new messianism made with human hands had been developed. Humanly speaking, one can understand the reason for this outburst of energy and the need for it. But though a limited understanding is shared, one cannot but fear that in the end a fatal mistake similar to the one that befell Babel will occur again. The determination to count only on self and to replace hope by human strength leads one also to imagine he can climb to the very gates of heaven on his own. The result inevitably is a terrible confusion, for man cannot replace God with impunity. In such a struggle life becomes a rat race, in which man loses sight of his mission and becomes lost in his self-constructed maze.

This process in which man destroys his God is a slow one. Step by step, according to an expression dear to Maurice Clavel, man "pushes God out of his life" and thus finds himself in a strange land. To use another word picture, man gets the habit of drinking from polluted sources and becomes so accustomed to "mixed waters" that he can even despise the rain from heaven.

Yet, for our time, for this very situation, an ancient message is waiting to be heard, clearing a stony path, announcing a new kingdom. Man has forgotten, perhaps, that God has spoken, that God has revealed the way, that He has promised to come!

So God Spoke

Once upon a time a people undertook a seemingly impossible adventure, marched into an unknown future with an unseen Guide, and struggled with One whom they could not see—that people was Israel.

This unusual encounter began an unusual history, from which was to emerge a very special Book. In those days God entered time and the words of men. Because God spoke, we believe in Him.

God is not a mythological hero. Before we were, He was. Divine reality, therefore, preceded human reality, and thus is even more sure. The Holy Scriptures were authored by men who were grounded on that reality. Real history produced the Book, not the reverse.

Influenced by literary criticism of the nineteenth century, some have thought to apply to the Bible a methodology essentially adapted to writings of a mythological or poetical nature. Those critics concluded that biblical accounts were simply sagas which had been put together in parable form to justify a rite or a commandment. That is, the ethical value or truth had created the story, according to this form of literary criticism.

But this principle of literary analysis, which was correct for writings like the *Iliad* and the *Aeneid,* created misunderstandings when used in biblical research. The Semitic mind is in sharp contrast with the Greco-Latin mind.[253] One takes a lesson from history; thus existence precedes thought. The other gets history from its morality, which means that thought precedes existence.

For the Hebrew, real experience with God produced a teaching, or, we would say, *is* a teaching. One cannot separate here flesh and spirit. In Hebrew, truth is inseparable from reality. So to say that the Bible is a collection of legends is, for a Hebrew, to discredit at the same time the Bible's message.

The prophet's conviction did not proceed from an intellectual or mystical impulse; rather it was nourished by the event. The Israelite did not write so he could be a poet or a philosopher and charm his readers. His song is a cry. His dialectic is an appeal. He spoke because he could not do otherwise.

Jeremiah writes: "O Lord, thou hast deceived me, and I was deceived. . . . If I say, 'I will not mention him, or speak any more in his name,' there is in my heart as it were a burning fire shut up in my bones, and I am weary with holding it in, and I cannot." Jeremiah 20:7-9.

Paul remembers: "I heard a voice saying to me in the Hebrew language, 'Saul, Saul, . . . It hurts you to kick against the goads.' " Acts 26:15.

The Hebrew prophet spoke because obligation was placed upon him to do so. The initiative was from the Spirit, which "pushed" him to deliver a message.[254]

This impetus—this weighty hand of the Spirit—which often meant suffering, is a sign that the prophet did not speak for himself on his own account. In no way was he an employee paid to give pleasure, to promise "fair days and blue skies" ahead. In appearance he was usually a man without commanding personality; yet he stood his ground, faced his people and the world, and proclaimed his message.

Jeremiah's lamentation was spoken one warm spring day. A throng had gathered to witness this strange tournament. A clash was to take place that would decide which of the two was right. Would it be Hananiah, son of Azzur, the well-known prophet from Gibeon, himself a distinguished personality; or would it be Jeremiah, a rejected scion of Abiathar and an inhabitant of the miserable little town of Anathoth?[255]

Hananiah spoke first, and his words were appreciated. He purred soothingly about peace and happiness. Everybody was reassured.

Then Jeremiah stood forth. His biting words tore at every heart. Bent down under his yoke, he shot back: "Amen! May the Lord do so. . . . Yet hear now this word which I speak in your hearing and in the hearing of all the people. The prophets who preceded you and me from ancient times prophesied war, famine, and pestilence against many countries and great kingdoms. As for the prophet who prophesies peace, when the word of that prophet comes to pass, then it will be known that the Lord has truly sent the prophet." Jeremiah 28:6-9.

Jeremiah's reasoning was without a flaw. Proof that he was speaking for God was that his message went contrary to his personal sentiments and those of the people and their leaders. He was clearly objective, even though it tormented the listeners. His words burned into hearts because they originated elsewhere and struck home. Such messages are to be compared to a "two-edged sword, piercing to the division of soul and spirit, of joints and marrow." Hebrews 4:12.

The Bible is not a book like all others. This has been said and resaid. But why has this been said and so recognized? The words of Scripture have been spoken ofttimes independently of the prophet's will—even against it. The prophet's inspired words cause men to change their direction and to move upward. Why can it be said that these words came from above? The reason lies within you! When God speaks, one is inclined to seek distraction, to play deaf, to march to another drummer. A message from God is disagreeable. Why? Simply because God's messages ask for a commitment.

The Fear of God

Here we come face-to-face with a paradox: One cannot hope to understand the revealed Word without committing oneself to follow in the path outlined by that Word. To understand Scripture, one pays a price; and that price is nothing short of one's very existence.

Too quickly has the Bible been relegated to the category of stories about "saints," of books fit only for children or the weak-minded. Nor should it be considered merely a source of comfort for the distraught. From another viewpoint, the Bible is often misunderstood by those who read and study it as much as it is by those who openly despise it.

Hence this unfortunate paradox, which only heightens perplexity. One is pleased, for the sake of publicity, to point out the influence of the Bible on Western culture and history. But in so doing, one can work against his argument and against the Bible.

To be sure, the Bible was the first book to be printed; and it remains the best seller, with approximately 35 million copies sold annually. To be sure, the Bible has been and remains the principal inspiration for poets, artists, philosophers, and even for men of state. But when this Western civilization is looked at carefully—this civilization that was fashioned so well by the Bible—and when one considers the many unhappy, disappointing aspects of this civilization and the unspeakable crimes that have been perpetrated by it, including the violation of man's most intimate and sacred possessions, there can be some question as to the nature of its influence, value, and authority.

The Bible has not really been heard by our civilization. Its words have resounded in people's ears but have not found an echo in their hearts and lives. Its words have influenced our language and culture but so little our personal existence and history. This is because the Word has not been seized upon by most men and women.

To understand the Word, one must incorporate it into life. Existence precedes thought. Thus, to believe in God and really to know Him, He must first be feared and loved. The risk lies in listening to and following His instructions. This fear of God is not just a vague feeling of superstition; it is at the same time an act of love and of obedience. It is remarkable, in fact, that the Bible has brought together these three ideas of fear, love, and obedience to God's commandments. [256] In Deuteronomy 10:12, 13, we find a clear parallelism portraying an equation wherein the "fear of God" equals "to love him" and "to keep his commandments." This is a very significant outline of Hebrew thought on this subject.

In the New Testament, John in particular continues this theme with the accent on love: "For this is the love of God, that we keep his commandments." 1 John 5:3; cf. 2 John 6; John 14:15. In the preceding verses, as an introduction, John mentions "fear"; but he goes on to eliminate any possible misunderstanding by stating that "perfect love casts out fear." 1 John 4:18. For John the references in Deuteronomy to "fear" were to be understood in the sense of "reverence."

By fearing God, which is to love Him and to keep His commandments, we can come to know Him and to enter into a personal relationship with Him. The knowledge of God belongs to the area of obedience to His commandments. John says it in so many words: "By this we may be sure that we know him, if we keep his commandments. He who says 'I know him' but disobeys his commandments is a liar, and the truth is not in him." 1 John 2:3, 4.

In a way, it is a rendezvous that God has set up. By advancing in harmony with His indications and in obedience to His counsel (commandments), man inevitably will meet Him somewhere along the path of life. At that moment our intelligence, our total being, will perceive His intentions and comprehend the dimensions of the Word now truly revealed. The Bible opens up to whoever takes it as it is.

The experience of fearing God[257] precedes the life of faith. To fear God is to believe that He sees us at every moment. Such an experience has no relationship, of course, with the so-called "terror" of the Old Testament, which some find pleasure in placing in opposition to the "grace" of the gospel. Fear of God is simply to believe that God exists—not merely off there in the blue yonder of the heavens, but nearby—that we never leave His sight. He cannot be deceived, because He sees all and knows and loves us intimately. You see, no-man's-land does not exist in love—no neutral ground, no "off limits," no clergy-laymen differentiations, no possibility for hypocrisy. Truth alone prevails; for this reason, God stays by us with a jealous love.[258] Nothing escapes His attentive eye, for it sees the depths of human conduct at all times and places. This is one of the major themes of the Bible.[259]

The corollary to this idea of the fear of God is the feeling of God's omnipresence—of His all-seeing eye. "The eye of the Lord is on those who fear him," proclaims the psalmist. Psalm 33:18. It is interesting to note that this association of ideas is found even in biblical language. The Hebrew word which conveys the idea "fear of God"[260] is related to the verb meaning "to see."[261]

The "fear of God"—a feeling that one is being seen—marks life with a religious dimension and a sensitivity for the sacred. It constrains one to make an effort, to respect self and also to respect others.

Because man has lost the consciousness of this divine eye, he often falls into disrespect for self and for others. By creating for himself an easy morality—his own—he has paradoxically ended up sacrificing his liberty, while his "soul" escapes from him unnoticed. This was expressed some time ago by Cardinal Daniélou: It is by "seeking to liberate oneself from the burdens of liberty [that] contemporary man has plunged headlong into servitude."[262]

Honor will be recovered only when man stands up and follows, though walking against the current, the commandments from above. Then he will resume his stately destiny: that of a religious being—upright and capable of finding again his God.

Between the Alpha and the Omega

The key to the biblical message is not in linguistics; nor is it even on the historical or theological plane. It is to be found on the existence level—

ours! To the degree that we put God at the beginning and at the end of all things, to that degree the Bible will speak and reveal itself to us.

It certainly cannot be by chance that the Bible has framed itself between two literal events. In the beginning of time "God created," and at the end of time "God will come." Be it the Hebrew Bible[263] only, or the Bible that contains both Testaments, the canon is so constituted that the first words are a reference to the Creation and the last words to God's coming.

John probably was thinking of this fact when he began his Gospel by mentioning the creative Word at the beginning (John 1:1-3) and concluded the Revelation, the last book of the New Testament, by invoking the kingdom of the Messiah (Revelation 22:20).

There must be, it would seem, a relationship between the two themes. We find them together in those ominous words pronounced by the angel in John's book of the Revelation—in words that precede the day of God's judgment, the day of His appearing: "He said with a loud voice, 'Fear God and give him glory, for the hour of his judgment has come; and worship him who made heaven and earth, the sea and the fountains of water.' " Revelation 14:7.

Note well that the angel's injunction to fear the God who made heaven and earth calls forth immediately the observance of the commandment which expresses that faith; that is, the Sabbath commandment.

"Remember the sabbath day, to keep it holy [set apart] . . . ; for in six days the Lord made heaven and earth, the sea, and all that is in them, and rested the seventh day; therefore the Lord blessed the sabbath day and hallowed it [set it apart]." Exodus 20:8-11.

The appeal recorded in the Revelation reminds us of a similar one in the book of Malachi. This Hebrew prophet also associates the announcement of the day of the Lord with an exhortation to remember the Law of Moses: "Remember the law of my servant Moses. . . . Behold, I will send you Elijah the prophet before the great and terrible day of the Lord comes." Malachi 4:4, 5 (3:22, 23 in the Hebrew Bible).

The passages in Malachi and the Revelation appear to echo each other. Both include the intervention of an angel (or messenger)[264] just before the day of God's judgment. Both passages are concerned with the great day of God's appearance or coming.

Both convey precise exhortation. The Malachi text asks that the Law of Moses handed down at Sinai be remembered; the Revelation text encourages fear of the Creator God.

The two passages may seem to differ only on this last point. But the analogy that exists suggests that there is a common preoccupation in the two passages. The language used and the ideas put forward reveal a like concern: the need of a return to the fourth commandment of the Decalogue.

In Malachi's text (1) the word *remember* recalls the *remember* of the Sabbath commandment;[265] (2) the "Law of Moses" that Moses proclaimed at Sinai recalls the Decalogue.

In the Revelation passage, (1) the "fear of God" recalls the observance of the commandments;[266] (2) the mention of Creation recalls the Sabbath which was to memorialize it.

The message that the Bible, including both the Old and the New Testaments, foresees as the very last announcement to the world is a picture with two panels: the observance of the Sabbath with reference to Creation, and an extraordinary proclamation on the coming of the Great Day of the Lord.

That these two "truths"—the Sabbath and the coming of the Lord—should be together in both the Old and New Testaments is not in the least astonishing; they simply express the same faith.

Respect for the Sabbath expresses faith in the God of Creation; that is, in a God capable of giving life. Only such a faith could accept the incredible fact (in human terms) of a re-creation, of a resurrection, and, as a consequence, of a new city to be structured and governed by God Himself. This faith alone can envision the true revolution: a total restructuring of this present world in order to establish a new one, in which will come together in a new way, end and origin, alpha and omega.

Respect for the Sabbath day, a memorial of Creation, and faith in the kingdom to come also create in the believer a profound dependence on God. The believer owes Him his origin and his destiny. Furthermore, when man sets apart a particular day, following God's direct order, he recognizes that God has the right to appropriate to Himself man's time.[267] Time then takes on a special dimension: a divine imprint. By tuning his week to the Law of heaven, man expresses his faith in something beyond daily contingencies; he places on time the seal of hope; he commits his existence totally to a "religion" without breaks or parentheses from his alpha to his omega!

Respect for the Sabbath day fixed by God and not for that other day chosen by the politics of men (although this replacement day sought justification later by theological arguments)[268] reveals to the believer the order to which he belongs: the order from above, the realm of the absolute, from which he draws his criteria. This means that many times he will have to swim against the currents of civilization that ultimately will carry him to perdition.

His kingdom is not of this world, either, but of God—of a God who is coming! Not that he entertains dreams beyond the realms of reality, for he does not. He simply wants his life here and now to be molded to the requirements sent down from above, to be radiant with the hope shining out of his future, to make sure that his alpha will stretch to his omega.

Thus a faith that respects the Sabbath and a faith that anticipates the final intervention from above are of the same nature. For this reason, these two truths represent the main theme of the Bible, summarizing its story from cover to cover. They also represent in substance that profession of faith par excellence in the God whom Scripture defines as "the beginning and the end," "the first and the last," "the alpha and the omega." Cf. Isaiah 44:6; 41:4; 48:12 and Revelation 1:8; 22:13.

Conversion Without Treason

Lekh lekha! Go!—God to Abraham.

A pilgrim in search of pure water pauses beside a fountain of bitter water. If he drinks from it, he runs the risk of poisoning his soul and his brother's so that he will no longer be able to accept mutual differences or listen to a different message. By drinking, he may come to the place where he will believe that he alone is right, that he somehow has been installed as God's only spokesman and right-hand magistrate. If he drinks of this bitter water, he risks a place in the hell of those who never thirst.

The pilgrim moves on. Suddenly a deep, majestic river flows swiftly before his eyes. Its beauty grips him, tempting him to make a permanent home on its bank. He notices that he would have a lot of company along its bank; it feels good to be with others, with family, surrounded by ancient habits and customs and traditions. But the river is polluted. It runs too close to the city. So it, like the bitter fountain, doesn't meet the needs of the pilgrim. "These waters are bound up with men," he muses; "but I must have water from on high if I am to survive."

The pilgrim must continue his travel. He walks, walks farther—

A true pilgrim never stops, because, headed for eternity, his existence is one of perpetual renewal. He decides to leave the throng of travelers, seeking out the ancient paths which had been lost. Conversion is his choice. No, not that despicable surrender, not that cowardly act that conversion often connotes!

A true, complete conversion is something else. It restores the converted one to his roots, recovers his ancient image, reconciles the creature with his Creator. Genuine conversion has been the purpose of biblical medita-

118

tion throughout its history. The Sacred Book owes its existence, in fact, to conversion.

Abraham, the father of the faithful, had to pass along that road. For him conversion was not easy. It involved, first of all, the sacrifice of his own past, which he admitted to have been vain, foolish, and false. Conversion required that he abandon his former habits of thought and conduct, which had been dear to him. It took him from his native land, from his customs, from his material and spiritual comforts. It rang a bell of departure and of a new beginning.

However, in this struggle solitude was the hardest test of all. Other trials remained constant, with little change. The same routine, the same road came with each rising sun. Thoughts, gestures, and work changed little. Could that be a kind of difficulty everyone on the conversion road experiences? It is difficult, too, to make changes—to be converted—because then one becomes different. And that difference is a heavy burden in the midst of people who are ever ready to condemn a stranger. Abraham had become the stranger, the permanent stranger, simply because he had been spoken to from on high and had answered Yes!

Some 2000 years later, Saul of Tarsus, the first and the greatest theologian produced by Christianity, had to go through the same experience. Pharisee and son of a Pharisee, he had studied at the feet of the great Gamaliel. He took pride in his lineage and training, and rightly so. A very decisive and determined man, Saul attacked and pursued people he considered to be dangerous heretics. He had the zeal of his convictions.

Yet, the day came when he, a doctor endorsed by Jerusalem, understood his mistake. Necessity forced him to sit again on the learner's bench. His life then changed. Henceforth he would travel from continent to continent in order to announce to the world the truth that had turned his life literally upside down. He was no longer the same well-organized official with an insured future. He set out upon the highways of the Greco-Roman world often not knowing where God would lead him, led only by his unshakable faith in the invisible. Once converted, Paul too became a stranger, bringing upon himself countless perils, including that of uncertainty. But his conversion also ushered in a strong faith in a God still ready to do the works of salvation.

Between these two men who became the chief human instruments of the Judeo-Christian revelation streams a vast people of strangers: Israel. The story of this people is nothing more than a story of perpetual conversion. Israel is not allowed to settle down in religion. To do so, becoming merely citizens of an earthly commonwealth, would be dangerous. Kings, priests, and prophets continually encouraged Israel to return to the old paths, exhorting the people to repent. Occasionally, the idols that had found their way into the habitations had to be destroyed. Other times, the purification of hearts was the chief concern. One only has to recall the revolutions brought about by a David, a Josiah, or a Nehemiah to get the full drift of Israel's story. The messages of Elijah the prophet, of Amos and Jeremiah, reveal the heart of Israel's destiny.

The people constantly were brought back to fundamentals. They never were allowed to settle down in an easy peace and compromise. Nor could they rest on the laurels of their ancestors. They had to take up the struggle every morning, renew constantly the covenant with God, sing daily a new song. It was not easy to be Israel, but it was thrilling! The mystery of Israel's election lay precisely in this never-ending conversion. Lectured to continuously, reprimanded unceasingly, Israel was constantly forced to call its very existence into question and to be ready always to make the needed correction: its conversion.

In the Bible conversion is represented as the highest possible life ideal. Possibly this is why nomadism is considered in Hebrew civilization as the outstanding virtue. The Levites, God's priests, were not permitted the right to put down roots anywhere. They thus made sure that material security would not blind their eyes to life's true values.

Israel as a whole had to undergo the teaching device of the desert, which later became a subject of nostalgia for the prophets. Hosea 2:16; Ezekiel 20:35-37. Those were the "good old days," when Israel, still a young betrothed, was experiencing the first love. Toward this spiritual golden age Israel's aspirations turned periodically when a special need for repentance and reconsecration was felt.

Whoever would follow in the biblical furrow must bend to this way of continual conversion. It is not primarily a question of passing from one religion to another—for a new baptism, for a betrayal of the faith. The point is simply to recognize, as did men and women of old, that one has lost his way. The need is for humility and courage to turn back, to consult the sources, to examine oneself, and to align oneself with the will of God. Conversion is not treason when it means to join up again with the fathers. Conversion is rather the fulfillment of the last prophecy of Malachi, who was to close the long line of Israel's prophets, a prophecy that concerns the time of the end, possibly ours:

"He will turn the hearts of fathers to their children and the hearts of children to their fathers." Malachi 4:6 (3:24 in the Hebrew Bible).

Epilogue

The Spirit Blows

Now that we have come to the end, we suddenly find that a doubt has invaded our thoughts—a feeling that perhaps we have run in vain.

Have we resolved the problems? Has the system we have attacked been at all shaken? Everything does seem to stand as before: superb, disdainful, weighted with a glorious past, strong in the strength of its leaders. After all, since when have mere words had the might to reverse history and to alter destiny? But did we not foresee this possibility at the threshold of our undertaking? Words and ideas couldn't possibly succeed.

So in despair one would be tempted to pray.

Of course, prayer is not in popular usage today. But we are not primarily concerned with an affair of fashion in keeping with times and cultures. The Spirit "blows where it wills" and when it wills. John 3:8.

So let the Spirit blow!

NOTES TO
DRINKING AT THE SOURCES

1. Samuel Joseph Agnon (1888-1970) is one of the greatest Hebrew writers of our time. His numerous works have won him international fame, confirmed by the Nobel Prize in literature in 1966.

2. "Le chien Balak" (French translation of *Tmol Chilchom*), p. 275.

3. Jules Isaac, *Genèse de l'Antisémitisme*, p. 148.

4. It is especially necessary to note the influence of the Jewish rebellions against the Roman Empire and the resulting persecutions of Judaism by the Roman emperors. Cf. Samuele Bacchiocchi, *Anti-Judaism and the Origin of Sunday* (Rome: 1975), pp. 37-39.

5. Marcel Simon, *Verus Israël*, p. 361, n. 4; F. Lovsky, *Antisémitisme et Mystère d'Israel*, p. 140.

6. Ignatius of Antioch, *Letter to the Magnesians* 9.1. The Greek text is susceptible to various translations, however, and one form of the text (that printed in the Migne *Patrologia Graeca*) indeed reads, "No longer sabbatizing, but living according to the *life* of the Lord."

7. Cf. Tertullian, *Against Marcion* 4.12.7.

8. Victorinus, *On the Creation of the World* 5 (*The Ante-Nicene Fathers* 7:342).

9. One finds the same concern at the Council of Nicaea (A.D. 325), when the issue came up in respect to Easter. Eusebius of Caesarea informs us of the emperor Constantine's opinion: "It appeared an unworthy thing that in the celebration of this most holy feast we should follow the practice of the Jews, who have impiously defiled their hands with enormous sin, and are, therefore, deservedly afflicted with blindness of soul. . . . Let us then have nothing in common with the detestable Jewish crowd." Eusebius, *Life of Constantine* 3.18-19 (*Nicene and Post-Nicene Fathers*, Second Series, 1:524-525).

10. Canon 29 of the Council of Laodicea. See Joannes Dominicus Mansi, ed., *Sacrorum Conciliorum Nova et Amplissima Collectio*, II, pp. 569-570.

11. Thus, among many other church historians, J.A.W. Neander has noted: "It was through opposition to Judaism that the feast of the Sunday was introduced very early in the place of the Sabbath." J.A.W. Neander, *Allgemeine Geschichte der Christlichen Religion und Kirche*, I, 2, p. 513.

12. Constantine's decree is clear: "The Emperor Constantine to A. Helpidius. All judges, townspeople and all occupations should rest on the most honorable day of the sun. Farmers indeed should be free and unhindered in their cultivation of the fields, since it frequently occurs that there is no more suitable day for entrusting

seeds of corn to the furrows and slips of vine to the holes prepared for them, lest haply the favorable moment sent by divine providence be lost." *Code of Justinian* III.12 (*de feriis*).3.

13. Pesiqta Rabbati 20.

14. Babylonian Talmud, Shabbath 88a.

15. On this question see Marcel Simon, *op. cit.*, p. 214 ff. and R. Travers Herford, *Christianity in Talmud and Midrash*.

16. Jules Isaac, *op. cit.*, p. 147.

17. Cf. in this connection Harnack's work, *Die Altercatio Simonis Judaei et Theophili Christiani, nebst Untersuchungen über die antijüdische Polemik in der alten Kirche,* Texte und Untersuchungen, 1, 3 (1883).

18. Marcel Simon, *op. cit.*, p. 437.

19. A. Neher, *L'Existence juive*, p. 236.

20. *Idem.*

21. It is noteworthy that the same distinctiveness in comparison to the church was already affirmed by Kimhi. (See F. E. Talmage, ed., *Disputation and Dialogue: Readings in the Jewish-Christian Encounter* (New York. Ktav Publishing House, Inc., 1975), p. 113. Abraham Heschel echoed him more precisely in connection with the Sabbath, which he defines as being "the idea that expresses what is most characteristic of Judaism" (*God in Search of Man*, p. 417).

22. *Op. cit.*, p. 203; cf. p. 96.

23. See J. Isaac, *op. cit.*, p. 146. Significantly, J. Parkes notices "the strange and tragic fact" that the Judeo-Christians were excommunicated by the Gentile Christians "not for an inadequate Christology, but because they still observed 'the law' " (*The Foundations of Judaism and Christianity*, p. 222).

24. From *Episcopal Orientation on Relations With Judaism* (IV, a).

25. Jean-Paul Sartre, *Anti-Semite and Jew*, p. 78.

26. On this, see Charles Herbert Stember and others, *Jews in the Mind of America*, pp. 48-59, and J.P. Sartre, *op. cit.*, pp. 63, 64.

27. Cf. the UNESCO report on the question, "Le racisme devant la Science" (Paris, 1973).

28. J.-P. Sartre, *op. cit.*, p. 23.

29. Albert Memmi, *Portrait d'un juif*, p. 203.

30. *Ibid.*, p. 154.

31. Cited by A. Memmi, *op. cit.*, p. 213.

32. Soren Kierkegaard, *Training in Christianity* (Princeton, 1944), pp. 176-178. For Kierkegaard, Christian pedagogy must on the contrary make the child understand his own culpability in the crucifixion. Moreover, he says explicitly, "This present generation must think that they themselves have crucified Him."

33. J. Isaac, *op. cit.*, p. 172.

34. Jules Isaac, *Jésus et Israël*, p. 558.

35. Albert Memmi, *La libération du juif*, p. 215.

36. *Ibid.*

37. This is the opinion of Hermann Gunkel, among others, who goes so far as to say that Abraham intended to sacrifice the honor of his wife in exchange for gifts. This exegesis, so current in Christian circles, partakes of an obvious bias. It simply does not take account of the facts given in the text, according to which Abraham was in danger of death. As for the expression "that it may go well with me because of you" (Genesis 12:13), it is in parallelism with "that my life may be spared on your account"; and it must be understood in the same sense (see also verse 12).

The difficult situation in which Abraham found himself explains his mistake, without, however, justifying it. Abraham is still with God through all the vicissitudes of his experience. We cannot but reproach him, however, for his lack of faith. Cf. Ellen White, *Patriarchs and Prophets,* p. 130; cf. also U. Cassuto, *A Commentary on the Book of Genesis,* pp. 348-352.

38. The Jewishness of Jesus has recently been pointed out by the Catholic theologian C. Tresmontant in *L'enseignement de Ieshoua de Nazareth.* Cf. also J. Klausner, *Jesus of Nazareth* (New York: Macmillan, 1942).

39. The role which the figure of Judas played in the Dreyfus affair is well known. "That Dreyfus is capable of treason," declared Barrès, "is something I conclude from his race." In the *Cività Cattolica* (February 5, 1898), a Jesuit periodical in Rome, one could read: "The Jews were created by a special decree of Providence in order that noble causes might not lack traitors." (Cf. Rabi, *Anatomie du Judaïsme français,* pp. 74, 75.)

40. Cf. *Genèse de l'Antisémitisme.*

41. That author had devoted a whole collection of works on *The History of Anti-Semitism* (English translation by Richard Howard, 1965): I. From the Time of Christ to the Court Jews; II. From Mahomet to the Marranos; III. From Voltaire to Wagner.

42. Cf. his two books, *Antisémitisme et mystère d'Israël* and *La déchirure de l'absence.*

43. As for works on anti-Semitism written in English, the following should be noted: Ernest L. Abel, *The Roots of Anti-Semitism* (1975); Heinrich J. M. Coudenhove-Kadergi, *Anti-Semitism Throughout the Ages* (1972); James W. Parkes, *Anti-Semitism* (1963). Note also the English translation of Jules Isaac, *The Teaching of Contempt.*

44. Pierre de Labriolle, *La Réaction païenne,* p. 194.

45. Staehelin, *Der Antisemitismus des Altertums,* p. 54.

46. In the Jewish review *L'Amandier fleuri* (October 1949), 9.

47. "Dimensions de l'antisémitisme," in *Foi et Vie* (September-October 1949), 447, 448.

48. J. Isaac, *Genèse de l'Antisémitisme,* p. 129.

49. Cf. *Verus Israel,* p. 263.

50. F. Lovsky, *Antisémitisme et mystère d'Israël,* p. 157.

51. M. Simon, *op. cit.,* p. 16.

52. J. Isaac, *op. cit.,* p. 133.

53. As one example, among others, we may cite this letter of the bishop of Agobard—a passage chosen from among the most violent of the epoch: "The men who are subject to the Mosaic Law are accursed and covered with the curse as by a garment, a curse which has soaked like water into their guts and like oil into their bones, cursed in the city and cursed in the field, cursed in their coming in and cursed in their going out. Cursed are the fruit of their body, of their ground, of their flocks, of their cellars, of their granaries, of their storehouses, of their sustenance and of the crumbs of their meals!" Letter to the archbishop of Narbonne, between A.D. 826 and 828; cited by J. Régné, "Les Juifs de Narbonne," *Revue des Etudes juives,* LV (1908), 34. (Cf. L. Poliakov, *The History of Anti-Semitism:* vol. I: *From the Time of Christ to the Court Jews,* pp. 29-30.)

54. "In many ways 1096 marked a turning point in Jewish history. The trail of blood and smoldering ruins left behind in the Jewish communities from France to Palestine. . . for the first time brought home to the Jewish people, its foes and

friends, the utter instability of the Jewish position in the Western world. . . . Jews had encountered occasional outbreaks of intolerance. . . . But these 'incidents' invariably were local and sporadic in nature and lacked premeditation and widespread concerted action. From the First Crusade on, anti-Jewish persecutions exercised a dangerously contagious appeal, which in periods of great emotional stress degenerated into a mass psychosis spilling over national boundaries." Salo W. Baron, *A Social and Religious History of the Jews*, vol. IV, p. 89.

55. Cf. A. Neubauer and M. Stern, *Hebrew Reports of the Persecutions of the Jews during the Crusades* (in Hebrew); German translation by S. Baer, *Hebräische Berichte über die Judenverfolgungen während der Kreuzzüge*, p. 88.

56. Contrary to the tenacious prejudice according to which the Jews were always those avaricious merchants and usurers, the documents reveal to us that before this date the divers expressions of anti-Semitism "know nothing of the avarice or economic greed of the Jews. When, in the mid fifth century, Salvian of Marseilles composed a treatise against avarice and usury, he never mentioned the Jews." F. Lovsky, *Antisémitisme et mystère d'Israël*, p. 233.

57. L. Poliakov, *op. cit.*, p. 74

58. See James Parkes, *The Jew in the Medieval Community* (London, 1938), p. 341. Cf. *Evidences* (May 1954), 22.

59. J. Parkes, *op. cit.*, pp. 340-341. Cf. J. Bernfeld, "Das Zinsverbot bei den Juden nach talmudisch-rabbinisch Recht," in *Das Licht*, No. 8.

60. F. Lovsky, *op, cit.*, p. 233.

61. "The loan of money . . . is the real motive for the tolerance of the lord who admitted the Jew, protected him, encouraged him, and then systematically exploited him and pitilessly fleeced him when the occasion presented itself, which was quite frequently." L. Gauthier, "Les juifs dans les deux Bourgognes," in *Revue d'Etudes Juives*, XLIX (1904), 14.

62. This feeling came to expression in some rather peculiar semantics. In the *Jewish Chronicles* of Solomon Bar Simeon or in that of Eliaz ben Nathan, the word *church* is thus regularly rendered by the term "place of impurity or of horror," the word *cross* by "evil sign," etc.

The *Hebrew Chronicles* have been published by A. Neubauer and M. Stern, *op. cit.*

63. It was the Lateran Council of 1215 which, by defining the status of the Jew as that of one outside the law, determined the formation of the ghetto. The phenomenon did not exist previously. It became obligatory from that moment on.

64. The Jew was considered the incarnation of evil, and he was held responsible for all evils (plague, etc.), and he would be identified with the devil, especially in the fourteenth century.

65. The expression is from Luther, who, after a notable friendliness toward the Jews during his earlier career, turned violently against them in his later period. (On this point see the monograph of Reinhold Lewin, *Luthers Stellung zu den Juden.*) Cf. Luther's pamphlet "Against the Jews and Their Lies": "In truth, the Jews, being foreigners, should possess nothing, and what they do possess should be ours." "To this day we still do not know what devil brought them into our country." "Aside from the Devil, you have no enemy more venemous, more desperate, more bitter, than a true Jew."

"On a practical level, Luther proposes a series of measures against the Jews: that their synagogues be burned and their books confiscated, that they be forbidden to pray to God in their own way, and that they be made to work with their hands; or, better still, that the princes expel them from their lands and that the authorities—magistrates as well as clergy—unite toward these ends. As for himself, having thus done his duty, Luther is 'excused.' (*Ich habe das meine gethan: ich bin entschuldigt!*) Poliakov, *op. cit.,* pp. 216-210.

In several passages, finally, Luther lamentably lets himself go into the most obscene buffoonery and gross vulgarities in lambasting the Jews, and he passes it all off as his most Christian sentiments.

66. "That was, in the seventeenth century, the weightiest reproach in Christian opinion." (F. Lovsky, *Antisémitisme et Mystère d'Israël,* p. 194.) The sermons of Bossuet hammered it into the ears of Christians: "That which the Romans found intolerable for their citizens, the parricidal Jews have inflicted upon their King" (*Sermon on the Virtue of the Cross,* in the Garnier edition, vol. III, p. 581).

67. As early as the Fourth Lateran Council it had been "decided that the Jews must distinguish themselves from the Christians by their dress." (Cf. Fourth Lateran Council, canons 67-70, in Mansi 22, pp. 1054 ff.)

68. See L. Poliakov, *The History of Anti-Semitism,* vol. III: *From Voltaire to Wagner.*

69. Cf. A. M. Rose, *L'origine des préjugés,* in the publications of the UNESCO, Paris, 1951, p. 15.

70. Cf. Ch. Lassen, *Indische Altertumskunde,* the conclusions of which were adopted by Ernest Renan. On this issue see the warning of Heinrich Coudenhove-Kadergi, *Anti-Semitism Throughout the Ages,* pp. 59-61.

71. "Among the Caucasian peoples, we must certainly give the palm to the Indo-Germans. We do not think that this is due to chance, but we believe that it must follow from their vastly superior talents. History teaches us that the Semites are not inclined to the harmonious balance of all the powers of the soul, which characterizes the Indo-Germans." Ch. Lassen, *op. cit.,* vol. I, p. 513.

72. As the historian Barraclough rightly observes regarding the movement of National Socialism, "They offered a solution—specious but boldly enunciated—not only of the immediate evil of unemployment, but also of the two great unsolved problems which stood out as the enduring legacy of Germany's past: the problem of German unity and the problem of creating political institutions representative of the German people." *Origins of Modern Germany,* p. 458.

73. H. Chamberlain, *La Genèse du XIXe siècle,* p. 362.

74. Cf. *Die Nibelungen, Allgemeine Geschichte* drawn from legend.

75. *Oeuvres en prose* de Richard Wagner, vol. II, pp. 44, 45, 56.

76. These sentiments echo the jibe of Luther's: "If I find a Jew to baptize, I shall lead him to the Elbe bridge, hang a stone around his neck, and push him into the water, baptizing him with the name of Abraham!" (Cited by L. Poliakov, *op. cit.,* I, p. 223.)

77. F. Lovsky, *La déchirure de l'absence,* p. 13.

78. Julian Green, *Journal,* in *Revue de Paris,* June 1949.

79. Cf. Psalm 119:105. *Torah* (law) and *Or* (light) come from the same Hebrew root.

80. Eusebius of Caesarea (ca. 330), a bishop contemporaneous with Constantine, says quite explicitly in his commentary on the Psalms, "On that day of light, the first day, day of the real sun, when we gather together at intervals of six days . . . we then accomplish, following the spiritual law, that which had been ordained by the law for the priests to do during the Sabbath . . . all that which had to be accomplished during the Sabbath we have brought over to the Lord's Day, inas-

much as it is the most important, the dominant, the first, and it has more value than the Sabbath." *Commentary of the Psalms,* on Psalm 91; see W. Rordorf, *Sabbat et dimanche,* pp. 79, 81.

Church historians have not failed to take note of this matter: "The Hebrew Sabbath having been abolished by Christians, the Church made a sacred day of Sunday, partly because it was the day of the resurrection, but largely because it was the weekly festival of the sun; for it was definite Christian policy to take over the pagan festivals endeared to the people by tradition, and to give them a Christian significance. But, as a solar festival, Sunday was the sacred day of Mithra; and it is interesting to notice that since Mithra was addressed as *Dominus,* 'Lord,' Sunday must have been 'the Lord's Day' long before Christian times." Arthur Weigall, *The Paganism in Our Christianity* (New York, 1928), p. 145.

81. A. Memmi, *Libération du Juif,* p. 73.

82. One may sometimes have the impression that the separation actually began in the time of the apostles. Reference is generally made to the declaration of St. Paul to his Jewish informers: "Behold, we turn to the Gentiles" (Acts 13:46). But in reality, the apostle indicates here quite simply that henceforth he would address himself *equally* to the pagans. The proof is that in the following chapter he is again preaching to the Jews. In any case, Paul's reaction in this verse concerns only a minority of Jews, as is clear from the preceding verses. In fact, the crowd which heard Paul's preaching was basically composed of Jews; and it was when they saw this crowd, the text says, that the other Jews "were filled with jealousy" (Acts 13:42, 43). There is reason to be astonished by such a contradiction in the same verse. But it is necessary to notice that in the New Testament the expression "the Jews" designates indistinctly either the friends or the enemies of Christ. (On this issue cf. Jules Isaac, *Jesus and Israel,* pp. 111-120; James Montgomery Boice, *The Gospel of John,* p. 14.) The second category of Jews, a minority, is rejected by Paul, but not the first category, which constitutes the majority. It is therefore essential, in order to avoid a misunderstanding, to take account of this verbal convention. Paul's sympathizers, as well as his persecutors, were Jews. Christ's disciples, as well as the instigators of His sacrifice, were Jews. We are all in Israel.

83. "A great and surprising revolution, deplored by some, praised by others, one of the most important in history, of which the reign of Constantine was only the prelude, which continued and was consummated by end of the century, the extraordinary and chaotic fourth century. But the unheard of fortune of the Church brought in its train the misfortune of the Synagogue: for the fourth century was a fatal epoch, which opened up a future of anguish, mourning, and catastrophes." Jules Isaac, *Genèse de l'Antisémitisme,* p. 156.

84. Isaac Bashevi Singer, cited by A. Memmi in *La libération du Juif,* p. 73.

85. *Ibid.,* p. 71.

86. Cf. Colossians 2:14. We shall study this question in greater depth in a later chapter (cf. p. 74 ff.).

87. Genesis 2:7. The word *nephesh,* which is usually translated "soul," and which is used equally for human beings or for animals (cf. Genesis 1:20), comes from the verb *naphash,* which means "to breathe" (cf. Exodus 23:12). Note its phonetic relationship with some other synonymous Hebrew verbs, such as *nachav, nacham* (to breathe). This word similarly has the meaning of "to breathe" in several other Semitic languages such as Akkadian and Arabic.

88. Genesis 3:15. This is our translation, intended to reflect the wordplay on the verb *shuf.*

89. Wisdom of Solomon 2:24.

90. Cassuto, A Commentary on the Book of Genesis, vol. I, pp. 142, 160.

91. Pentateuch with Targum Onkelos, Haphtaroth and Prayers for Sabbath and Rashi's Commentary, Translated into English and annotated by Rev. M. Rosenbaum and Dr. A. M. Silbermann in Collaboration with A. Blashki and L. Joseph: Genesis (London: Shapiro, Vallentine and Co., 1946), p. 15.

92. This Greek version is the oldest Jewish translation still extant. It dates from the third century B.C.E.

93. The use of the personal pronoun autos for the subject that would bruise the serpent's head is significant for us: since it is a masculine nominative pronoun it can refer neither to the woman, nor even to the posterity ("seed") collectively, which is a neuter word in Greek.

94. Even some modern commentaries do not hesitate to interpret this verse in a Messianic sense (cf. Marc Breuer, Thora commentée, p. 15).

95. The Targums are ancient paraphrastic translations of the Scriptures into Aramaic.

After the return from the Captivity (539 B.C.E.), Aramaic replaced Hebrew as the vernacular language of the Jewish people. The biblical texts which were read as part of the liturgy survived because the people understood them when they were interpreted in Aramaic, hence the Targums. These were not simply translations, for they comprised virtual commentaries, reflecting the religious ideas of the time. The two best-known Targums are those of Onkelos on the Pentateuch (second century C.E.) and that of Jonathan on the Prophets (third century C.E.).

96. See its commentary on Genesis 3:15.

97. See its commentary on Genesis 3:15. This Targum, attributed to Jonthan (see note 95) bears on the Pentateuch and the Hagiographa. Redacted in the Palestinian dialect of Aramaic, it was called the Targum of Jerusalem, in contrast to the other Targum of Jonathan, which was redacted in the Babylonian dialect and which was concerned only with the Prophets.

98. This work was formerly attributed to Rabbi Simeon ben Yohai, a Palestinian rabbi of the second century. It is now known that it was written in Spain in the thirteenth century. It constitutes the masterwork of Jewish mysticism, the Kabbalah.

99. Zohar, vol. II, folio 120b.

100. Gematria was a haggadic method of interpretation based on the numerical value of the letters.

101. Cf. Isaiah 52:13 with chapter 53.

102. The Talmud is a compilation of debates, interpretations, and scriptural commentaries covering roughly the period from the fourth century B.C.E. to the fifth century C.E.

The Talmud consists of a basic text, the Mishnah (teachings transmitted orally since the fourth century B.C.E. and put into writing in the second century C.E.) and the commentary upon it, the Gemara.

In this way, and in this format, there came into being two Talmuds: the Gemara of the Babylonian Rabbis gave birth to the Babylonian Talmud, and the Gemara of the Palestinian Rabbis produced the Jerusalem Talmud.

The Babylonian Talmud is by far the most important. It is for that reason that we generally mean that Talmud when we refer to the "Talmud." When we refer to the Jerusalem Talmud it will be specifically indicated by the abbreviation T. J.

103. Sanhedrin 98b. (This and similar references are to the Babylonian Talmud,

which consists of sixty-three books, or "tractates," of which Sanhedrin is one. The rest of the reference indicates the folio number and the side, or column, of the folio—each folio, or sheet, having two sides of columns.)

104. The term *Midrash* is applied to a certain number of compilations in which the various books of the Bible are expounded by means of the ancient traditions and by parables. They, like the Talmud, belong to the oral law and go back to roughly the same time period.

105. Pesiqta Rabbati, Pisqa 37.

106. Bereshith Rabbati of Moshe Hadarshan, on Genesis 24:67.

The same verse (Isaiah 53:5) is taken up in another Midrash to support its Messianic reading of the book of Ruth: "These words apply to King Messiah: 'come here' (in Ruth 2:14) means King of the Kingdom, and 'eat some bread' implies the Bread of the Kingdom, and 'dip your morsel in the wine' alludes to the suffering which is spoken of in Isaiah 53:5 when it says, 'he was bruised for our iniquities' " (Ruth Rabbah, 5:2:14). Ruth Rabbah is one of the component works in the Midrash Rabbah, a midrashic commentary on ten biblical books.

107. It is interesting to note that the root KRB, from which derives the word *Korban*, "sacrifice," expressed the idea of proximity and that the verb "to sacrifice," *hakrib*, formed from the same root by inflexion in the Hiphil (causative) stem, in fact signifies "to bring near." Therefore only the context can determine whether it is to be translated "sacrifice" or "bring near."

Thus Jeremiah 30:21 poses a problem of translation. It concerns a chief, a leader who will come forth from the womb of Israel; "I will make him draw near," says verse 21. Now, the verb used here is precisely that which is used for the Levitical cult; and it could be translated: "I will sacrifice him." It is followed by the verb *nagash* ("to have access to").

One encounters the same association between *hakrib* and *nagash* in Leviticus 21:21, which employs the verb *hakrib* in the sense of "sacrifice."

The verse in Jeremiah could therefore be rendered thus: "I will sacrifice him and one will thus have access to me" (the second verb is impersonal).

This translation has the merit of taking account of the words which follow: "For who would dare of himself to approach Me?" In fact, according to the Levitical theology only sacrifice makes God accessible to man (cf. Genesis 4:4; Leviticus 4).

108. Zebahim 44b and Sanhedrin 51b.

109. Leviticus 4:31.

110. Leviticus 4:34, 35; 16.

111. Leviticus 16:32-34.

112. Leviticus 16:14.

113. Exodus 28:35.

114. Aboth de Rabbi Nathan 34.

115. Bereshith Rabbati on Genesis 14:18.

116. Cf. Sukkah 52a. This is the only passage in all the Talmud which speaks of two Messiahs. It is possible therefore to think that we have here a late addition contemporaneous with the Midrashim and with the Jewish apocalypses, which reflect the Jewish-Christian polemics.

117. Cf. Joseph Klausner, *The Messianic Idea in Israel,* pp. 129, 400-401.

118. Sanhedrin 98b.

119. Bereshith Rabbati on Genesis 24:67.

120. Bereshith Rabbati on Genesis 19:34; cf. Berakoth 5a, etc.

121. Pesiqta Rabbati, Pisqa 37.

122. Targum on Song of Songs 4:5 and 7:3.

123. Sanhedrin 98b.

124. Cf. A. Sarsowsky, *Die ethisch-religiöse Bedeutung der alttestamentlischen Namen nach Talmud, Targum und Midrasch.*

125. Abraham Joshua Heschel, *God in Search of Man*, p. 137.

126. *Ibid.*, p. 412.

127. Often what the biblical passage understands from a messianic perspective is concerned equally with a particular historical situation. But the circumstantial interpretation does not exclude the messianic application. Generally speaking, it is the political salvation of Israel, on the occasion of its return from the Exile, which incidentally calls forth an allusion to a greater and deeper salvation—that which would be achieved by the Messiah. We are here confronted by a conception of time peculiar to the Hebrew mind, whereby two different epochs are embraced by one glance. What happens is that the inspired prophet in vision transcends his own time so as to enter into the time of God, which calls him. See André Neher, *Essence du prophétisme*, pp. 83 ff.

128. This is the common designation of God in the Rabbinic literature.

129. Baba Bathra 75b.

130. Lamentations Rabbah 1:1:16; Midrash on Proverbs 19:19-21; Midrash on Psalm 21:1, 2, etc.

131. Targum on Jeremiah 23:5, 6.

132. Pesiqta de Rab Kahana, Pisqa 28.

133. Targum on Isaiah 9:5.

134. Genesis 49:8-12.

135. This probably comes from the word *shalwah*, which means peace, serenity. Zadok Kahn translates the name "the Peaceful One."

136. Sanhedrin 98b; the Midrashim frequently refer to this verse: Lamentations Rabbah 1:1:16; Midrash Hagadol 158, etc.; Bereshith Rabbati on Genesis 49:10. This last passage identifies the star that comes out of Jacob, prophesied by Balaam in Numbers 24:17, with this Shilo, i.e. the Messiah.

137. Cf. Psalm 2:6-10.

138. Sukkah 52a.

139. Exodus Rabbah 8:1, on Exodus 7:1 (Soncino edition, p. 115). Exodus Rabbah is one of the component works in the Midrash Rabbah, a series of ten midrashic commentaries on as many books of the Bible, viz., the five books of Moses (Genesis, Exodus, Leviticus, Numbers, and Deuteronomy), and the five Scrolls read publicly on the major Jewish festivals (Song of Songs, Ruth, Lamentations, Ecclesiastes, and Esther). They are sometimes referred to by their Hebrew names; thus Exodus Rabbah may be called Shemoth Rabbah. These works are divided into traditional chapters and sections, which do not necessarily correspond to the chapters and verses of the biblical books being expounded. The standard English translation is published by the Soncino Press, but there are variant texts.

140. Cf. Isaiah 11:1-6.

141. Genesis Rabbah 2:4, on Genesis 1:2 (Soncino ed., p. 17).

142. The seed or shoot is one of the most dominant images in the Rabbinic literature for evoking the person of the Messiah (cf. T. J. Berakoth 5a; some texts of Numbers Rabbah 18, on Numbers 15:35; Genesis Rabbah 23:5, on Genesis 4:25, Soncino p. 196; in the latter midrash, King Messiah is conceived as "that seed which would arise from another source").

143. Bereshith Rabbati, on Genesis 37:22.

144. Tehillim Rabbati (Rabbi Mosheh Hadarshan) on Psalm 85:12.

145. Parallelism is a literary device which consists of making words, entire phrases, or even chapters correspond to each other in a variable process of reciprocal reference.

It is explained basically by that primitive tendency of the Hebrew mind to harmonize form with substance. The Hebrew verb follows closely the outpouring of thought and feeling and thus gives the impression of an impulsive discharge by successive surges.

The fact is that it unfolds in a concentric manner and in that way is led to repeat the same theme, to specify it, to develop it, and to compass it in all its aspects.

Parallelism is, however, a form of elaborate repetition which follows rather precise rules. It answers to several techniques which are attested in the Bible and which we find in all the literature of the ancient Middle East, notably in that of Ugarit:

(1) The *simple* method. The second stich repeats the first in synonymous terms (Genesis 4:23); see Isaiah 27:1, above p. 47.

(2) The *synthetic* or *complementary* method. The second stich completes the idea of the first (Psalm 1:2); see Daniel 9:24, pp. 63, 64.

(3) The *antithetic* method. Two contrary expression are placed together in order to make them produce a contrast (Proverbs 10:1); see Micah 4 and 5, on pp. 56, 57.

(4) The *chiastic* or *criss-cross* method. The two expressions criss-cross each other, suggesting the form of the Greek letter Chi, (Genesis 9:6); see Micah 4:8 and 5:3b; 5:1; 4:14, on pp. 63, 64. Daniel 9:25-27, p. 65.

(5) The *progressive* method. The same thought is expressed in a manner increasingly more and more intense and more specific (Psalm 29:1); see Daniel 9:25, 26, on p. 65.

The importance of parallelism is considerable. It undeniably plays a major role in understanding the meaning of the biblical writings. Even the meaning of the words can be shaded or changed under the influence of parallelism. In order to understand a text, it is therefore absolutely indispensable to determine before everything else its literary structure and thereby to reveal the parallelisms which run through it.

It was not until the eighteenth century that attention was given in Christian circles to the esthetic characters of Hebrew poesy. Particular credit is due to the Anglican bishop R. Lowth for having placed emphasis for the first time on the importance of parallelism (his work was published in 1753 in Latin, then reissued in English under the title *Lectures on the Sacred Poetry of the Hebrews).*

His work was, however, anticipated by the work of Jewish exegetes, among whom special mention is due to David Kimhi, Levi ben Gershom, and above all to Abraham ibn Ezra. (In an earlier epoch, Philo of Alexandria and Flavius Josephus had already discussed and studied this question; but their observations were strongly influenced by the metrical canon of the Greeks, as were those of Origen, Eusebius, and Jerome.) Afterward, research progressed to the point where we would not think of studying the Bible seriously while ignorant of such an important principle (cf. especially articles on Hebrew poetry in the better Bible dictionaries: G. B. Gray, *The Forms of the Hebrew Poetry;* Martin Buber, *Schriften zur Bibel,* which has the merit of assessing all the import of parallelism for exegesis).

146. This is equally the case with Genesis 1 and 2 (cf. U. Cassuto, *La questione della Genesi,* p. 258).

147. T. J. Berakoth 5a.

148. Bereshith Rabbati, on Genesis 49:10.

149. Cf. the Targum of Jonathan in its version of the passages—see especially verses 4:7-8 and 5:1.

150. Cf. Yoma 10a, Sanhedrin 18b, Sukkah 52b, Song of Songs Rabbah 8, etc.; Targum of Jonathan on Micah 4:7, 8; Micah 5:1; etc.

151. Genesis Rabbah 56:16; cf. also Midrash on Psalm 126:3.

152. A. and R. Neher, *Histoire Biblique du Peuple d'Israel,* p. 305.

153. Cf. Genesis 22.

154. Cf. 1 Chronicles 21:15, 16.

155. Cf. 1 Chronicles 21:28 to 22:1.

156. Aboth de R. Nathan 34.

157. Philo, *Legum allegoria,* III.79-80 (Loeb ed., vol. I, p. 353).

158. Baba Bathra 75b. Cf. Midrash on Psalm 21:1—"Just as He names the Messiah by His own name, so will He also name Jerusalem by His own name."

159. Cf. 2 Kings 9 and Hosea 1:4.

160. For the dialectic between Jerusalem and Bethlehem, see the parallelism in Micah, above on pp. 56, 57.

161. Sanhedrin 98a.

162. For his coming on the foal of an ass, see Baruch Rab, section 13 on Genesis 32:5; Tanhuma on Genesis 32:5; etc.

For his coming "on" the clouds, see Numbers Rabbah 13:13-14.

163. Cf. note 145 on parallelism.

164. The Masoretic marginal reading proposes for the first proposition the reading HTM and not KHTM, as the written text indicates. However that may be, the meaning would hardly be different (to put an end) and the wordplay would be nevertheless preserved.

165. The holy of holies (*qodesh qodashim*) is the technical term which in the Hebrew Bible designates this apartment of the Temple (cf. Exodus 26:33, 34).

166. This refers to the covering of the Ark of the Covenant, the box or chest containing the tables of the Law (cf. Exodus 4:20; Deuteronomy 10:1-5).

167. The proof is that lamentation for the destruction of the Temple which is reported to us in the Talmud: "Woe to the peoples; great is their ruin. They do not know what they have lost. While the Temple stood, the altar made expiation for them. Henceforth who will do it?" (Sukkah 55b).

168. The expression *ayn lo* appears to be a contraction of the expression which is found elsewhere in the book of Daniel (Daniel 11:45): *ayn ozer lo,* and which means "no one to help him."

169. This punctuation goes back to the tenth century of our era.

170. The Peshitta is a translation in the Syriac language written about the second century A.D.

171. That this paragraph can only refer to the Messiah can be seen by the following observations: (1) the presence of the theme of the weeks, a key word associated with the Messiah; (2) its conformity to the chiastic pattern of the passage (Messiah—Jerusalem—Messiah—Jerusalem—Messiah—Jerusalem); (3) finally, the ideas of covenant (Berith) and of cessation of offerings (Yashbit), taking up the ideas expressed through the verb *ykaret* of the preceding messianic paragraph (A1), constituting therefore an additional indicator according to which A2 is arranged on the same plan as A1 and continues it. The word KRT (cut off) is in fact an allusion at the same time to the covenant (KRT is precisely the technical word which expresses the ratification of the covenant; cf. Exodus 24:8; 34:27; Joshua 9:15;

133

Hosea 2:20; Jeremiah 34:13; etc.) and to the cessation. The word *ykaret* already contains in A₁ the two theological meanings of the death of the Messiah—which we found explained in A₂ as confirming the covenant by His sacrifice—and at the same time of the end of the sacrifices.

172. This mode of interpretation is also found in the Essene writings of the Dead Sea manuscripts. The seventy weeks are in these writings converted to 490 years, a period they also have terminating at the coming of the "Teacher of Righteousness":

"But remembering the Covenant of the Patriarchs, He left a remnant to Israel. . . . And in the time of wrath, three hundred and ninety years [a note by Dupont-Sommer in the work from which this translation is taken explains how in this document the total time period actually meant is really 490 years] after He had delivered them into the hand of Nebuchadnezzar king of Babylon, He visited them. . . . And He raised up for them a Teacher of Righteousness to lead them in the way of His heart and to make known to the last generations what He would do to the last generation." The Damascus Covenant (also known as the Zadokite Document) 1:4-11; translation from A. Dupont-Sommer, *The Essene Writings From Qumran*, translated by Geza Vermes, pp. 121-122.

173. Nazir 32b.

174. Yoma 54a.

175. Lamentations Rabbah 34.

176. Some have thus supposed that it is a question of two different Messiahs in the passage. But nothing in our text authorizes such an explanation. Both times there is the same term of Messiah, in the same indefinite grammatical form, which is employed with several intervening words. As for the word *Nagid* (prince), which qualifies the first occurrence of the word Messiah, it simply indicates his princely ascendancy according to the old messianic tradition (cf. Genesis 49:10).

The fact that this qualifying word does not occur the second time ought not to be taken into consideration in order to conclude that the author is abruptly speaking of a new Messiah. It is as if one spoke in the same paragraph, first of a beautiful tree and then a second time of a quite short tree; it is evident that it still remains a statement about the same tree.

177. Cf. note 172.

178. The date which the biblical account provides for the decree of Artaxerxes is pinpointed in Ezra 7:8. It is the moment when Ezra arrives in Jerusalem and finally announces to Israel the terms of the decree, and this became effective from that time on. This brings us "to the fifth month of the seventh year of Artaxerxes."

History informs us that Artaxerxes began to reign from the year 465 B.C.E. That is the year of his accession to the throne. Now, for the Bible, the first year of a reign is actually counted from the beginning of the following year (see Jeremiah 25:1 and Daniel 1:1, 2; cf. 2 Kings 18:1, 9, 10).

Moreover, the years of the reign were counted in the Bible beginning with the autumn (month of Tishri), following the practice of the Persian system then in force. This explains why, for example, in Nehemiah 1:1 and 2:1 the month of Nisan (first month) is preceded by Kislev (ninth month), all the time referring to the same twentieth year of the reign of Artaxerxes (the traditional Jewish calendar begins with Passover in the month of Nisan; then come the months of Iyyar, Sivan, Tammuz, Ab, Elul, Tishri, Heshvan, Kislev, Tebeth, Shebat, and Adar).

For the Mishnah as well as the Talmud, the year of reign in the Bible must begin in Tishri (cf. Mishnah, Rosh haShanah 1:1 and T.B. Rosh haShanah 3:72; cf. also the commentary in Hebrew of Hartom-Cassuto on the verse in Nehemiah 1:1).

And since Artaxerxes acceded to the throne in 465, it is necessary to place his first regnal year from the autumn of 464 to the autumn of 463 and his seventh year therefore from autumn 458 to autumn 457. It is precisely in the fifth month, Ezra tells us, that the decree was promulgated. The first month was that of Nisan (month of the Passover; see Ezra 6:19); so the fifth month takes us to Ab: *it is the end of the summer of 457 B.C.*

179. The use of the verb *ykaret* is very suggestive in this connection. The verb is regularly used in the Bible to designate the execution of an offender (cf. Numbers 15:31; Leviticus 20:17), or, in a broader sense, a massacre (cf. Isaiah 11:13; Micah 5:8).

180. Flavius Josephus, *Jewish Antiquities* 10.11.7.

181. Flavius Josephus was born A.D. 37.

182. Josephus, *ibid.*

183. Berakoth 12b.

184. Even circumcision could be interpreted in this sense. Subsumed under the idea of sacrifice, it appeared in the Old Testament as having the effect of appeasing the anger of God.

This is the explanation of the episode concerning Moses (the "bloody husband"), threatened with death by God simply because he had neglected to practice circumcision (cf. Exodus 4:24-26).

In that way of thinking we can also explain the relation between circumcision and the Passover lamb—symbol of the grace of God which "passes over" (cf. Exodus 12:43-49; Joshua 5:2-9).

Finally, by striking man in the place where the vital seed resides, circumcision evokes the Person of the Creator. This relationship has been noted in the Mishnah: "Great is circumcision, for without it the world would not have been created" (Nedarim 3:11).

According to this last interpretation, circumcision would be an allusion to the ultimate rending of the Creator, who did not hesitate, in order to save man, to "mutilate" His very Self.

As a matter of fact, the Hebrew word *Berith Milah* would already suggest such an interpretation. *Berith Milah* means "the covenant of cutting," or more precisely, the "cutting of cutting," which is a superlative, the cutting *par excellence.*

Beyond circumcision we can catch a glimpse of the various aspects of the Messianic ministry: sacrifice, rending, covenant, etc., at the level of the very Person of the Creator.

185. *Jewish Antiquities* 18.3.3. The passage is considered to be among the most securely authentic by all scholars, whether Jewish or Christian (cf. Ch. Guignebert, *Jesus*, pp. 16-17, and J. Klausner, *Jesus of Nazareth*, pp. 55-57).

186. Luke 3:1, 23. According to this passage, Jesus began His ministry in the fifteenth year of the reign of Tiberius Caesar, from the moment when He was baptized and anointed (*meshiah*) by the Spirit of God (cf. Luke 3:21, 22).

That fifteenth year must be counted beginning in 765 (year 12 in our reckoning), the date of which Augustus caused it to be voted by the Senate and the Roman people as the law of the empire that Tiberius would be his equal at the head of the Roman Empire. Archaeology has confirmed this date, since some coins have been discovered at Antioch bearing the date 765 of the Roman calendar and reproducing the likeness of Tiberius with an inscription of the significant expression, "Kaisar Sebastos."

Furthermore, the Syrian calendar, which we have reason to believe was the one followed by Luke, made the regnal year begin in autumn, just as the Israelites of the Old Testament had done (cf. *Dictionnaire encyclopédique de la Bible*, article "Chronologie du Nouveau Testament"). The fifteenth year of Tiberius therefore extends from the autumn of 779 to the autumn of 780 of the Roman era, i. e., *from autumn 26 to autumn 27 of our era.*

Finally, it must be remembered that the monk Dionysius Exiguus, who is the originator of our chronological reckoning, erroneously fixed the beginning of the Christian era at January 1, year 754 of the Roman era, which was four years after the birth of Christ. The Gospels inform us, in fact, that Christ was born a few months before the death of Herod, which happened in the year 4 before the common era (cf. Matthew 2:1, 15, 19 ff.; cf. Emil Schürer, *Geschichte des jüdischen Volkes*, part 1, pp. 415-417; and Josephus, *Jewish Antiquities* 17.8.1; *The Jewish War* 1.33.1), which explains how Jesus could be about thirty years of age in the year 27.

It can therefore be affirmed with certainty that Jesus' thirtieth year easily falls within the fifteenth year of the reign of Tiberius, as the third chapter of Luke gives us to understand, and as already mentioned. Actually, taking account of the fact that Jesus was born in the fourth year before the Christian era (the year of the death of Herod, as mentioned), he was about thirty years old in the period which covers from autumn 26 to autumn 27, and that period corresponds, as we have seen, to the fifteenth year of Tiberius.

But at what exact moment of the year did the baptism of Jesus take place? According to the seventy weeks prophecy, that would have had to be in the autumn of 27. If the data of the Gospels permit us to be sure as to the year, they leave us, by contrast, in the area of hypothesis as to the precise moment in that year. This is the only detail for which the verification of the Seventy Weeks leaves something to be desired. But when one takes account of the perfect correspondence of all the rest, there can be little doubt of the reliability and high value of the prophecy.

187. Cf. Ed. Fleg, *Jésus raconté par le juif errant*, p. 21. Cf. Sanhedrin 97b; Luke 2:25, 26.

188. According to the Gospels, Jesus celebrated the Passover four times (cf. John 2:13; 5:1; 6:4; 13:1).

189. Cf. Ch. Guignebert, *Jesus*, p. 21; cf. H. L. Strack, *Jesus, die Häretiker und die Christen nach den ältesten jüdischen Angaben.*

190. By his real name, Loeb, Judah ben Bezaleel (1512-1609)—eminent Talmudist, Cabbalist, scholar, and thinker—the Maharal of Prague is still famous because of his important literary and philosophical work. Numerous studies have been devoted to him (cf. A. Neher, *Le puits de l'exil;* B. Gross, *Le messianisme juif;* Th. Dreyfus, *Dieu parle aux hommes*).

191. Cf. Tipheret, chapter 29.

192. Samson R. Hirsch, *Ten Letters on Judaism*, No. 18. Hirsch was a German rabbi who became the champion of Orthodox Judaism in opposition to the Reform movement and assimilationism.

193. See his drama, *Nathan the Wise.*

194. *La Racine et la Source*, p. 122. The Church historian Leonhard Goppelt has recognized this point: "Thus Jesus' disciples did not consider themselves, as did the Essenes and Pharisees, to be the *True* Israel who were soon to inherit salvation. Rather they considered themselves to be the *New* Israel upon whom God's salvation had already dawned, even though the word 'new' was not expressed at first. Unlike the others they did not disparage the Jewish nation outside their own fellowship,

but addressed it as a whole, just and unjust alike, and emphasized its being the people of the promise." Goppelt, *Apostolic and Post-Apostolic Times,* translated by Robert A. Guelich, p. 28; cf. p. 14.

195. *Le Judaïsme,* p. 74.

196. The Greek verb *pl'er'osai* is the opposite of *katalusai,* to unloose, to destroy, to overthrow; and it comes from the root *pl'er'es,* full, which justifies Jules Isaac's translation, "to give fulness" (cf. J. Isaac, *Jésus et Israël,* pp. 65, 66). The *Today's English Version* brings out another nuance.

197. *L'enseignement de Ieschoua de Nazareth,* p. 122.

198. Shabbath 128a.

199. *L'enseignement de Ieschoua de Nazareth,* p. 122. Cf. also Burton Scott Easton, *Christ in the Gospels,* pp. 82-139.

200. "The scribes and the Pharisees sit on Moses' seat," affirmed Jesus, "so practice and observe whatever they tell you!" This he said to his disciples. (Matthew 23:2, 3.)

If Jesus had really advocated the annulment of the Law, then none of His followers would have understood His teaching—not even His mother, Mary. In fact, do we not see her, after the death of her Son, resting on the Sabbath, "according to the Law"? (Cf. Luke 23:56 and 24:10.)

201. The examples chosen to illustrate his thesis are taken from the Decalogue: "Thou shalt not commit adultery . . . thou shalt not kill" (James 2:11).

202. The American Catholic theologian Gregory Baum has been struck by this seeming contradiction in the epistles of Paul concerning the Law. "One of the most difficult theological notions in the letters of St. Paul," he tells us, "is that of the Law. It is obscure and puzzling because it seems to contain certain contradictions, attitudes opposed to one another to such a degree that they apparently defy an attempt at reconciliation. On the one hand we hear that the Law is good. . . . While quotations from Paul confirming the holiness of the Law could be multiplied, there exists also a sizeable set of passages which manifest a negative evaluation of the Law." *The Jews and the Gospel* (London, 1961), p. 186.

203. Cf. Deuteronomy 10:1-5 and 31:25, 26. The first passage mentions tablets of stone (cf. also Exodus 25:16; 40:20; and 1 Kings 8:9), the second, a book. As it happens, it was a book which was rediscovered in the Temple some 900 years later in the time of King Josiah (cf. 1 Chronicles 34:15, 31). The book deposited at the side of the ark dealt with the sacrifices. It is of further interest that it was to those who officiated at the sacrifices that the book was entrusted (cf. Deuteronomy 31:9).

204. The Hebrew word *Teshub,* which translates the idea of repentance, literally means "a turning back."

205. "What can be substituted for the oxen which we used to offer unto Thee? Our lips, with the prayer which we offer unto Thee." Pesiqta 165b. Cf. Hebrews 13:15.

206. *L'enseignement de Ieschoua de Nazareth,* pp. 137, 138. Cf. also F. Lovsky, *La déchirure de l'absence.)*

207. Page 129. On the Jewish side, note especially the works of Sch. Ben Chorin, *Bruder Jesus: Der Nazarener in jüdischer Sicht;* David Flusser, *Jesus;* and other authors such as Joseph Klausner, Salomon Asch, R. Aron, etc.

208. *Revue Biblique* (1910), p. 10.

209. The Jewish historian Leon Poliakov underlines this fact vigorously: "Nothing in the teaching of the Nazarene, even though it could shock many a doctor of the Law, constituted a formal heresy from the Jewish point of view." *The History of*

210. On this occasion they had scorned the most respected customs of Jewish jurisprudence. In fact, the Talmud informs us that no trial, and especially no trial involving an alleged capital offense, could be conducted on the eve of the Sabbath or a festival (Cf. Sanhedrin 4:1; cf. Lagrange, *John,* p. 471). Likewise, they despised the Mishnaic principle that "trials in which the life of a man is at stake must take place in the light of day." (Cf. Daniel-Rops, *Jesus and His Times,* p. 490.)

211. John 19:6. According to the same source, it was also the priests who had answered Pilate with the words "We have no king but Caesar" (John 19:15), which harmonizes perfectly with the data of history. The priests felt a greater degree of solidarity with the Roman power than with the common people (see next note).

212. Nominated by the Roman governor, they were in fact captive to him. They retained no power—not even that of inflicting capital punishment (cf. Mishnah Sanhedrin 1:1; 7:2). They were even more stringently dependent on the Roman procurator because he kept custody, under lock and key, of their sacerdotal vestments and ornaments. (Cf. Jules Isaac, *Jésus et Israël,* p. 274.)

213. Flavius Josephus, *Jewish Antiquities* 20.8.

214. This refers to the family of Caiaphas.

215. J. Klausner, *Jesus of Nazareth,* p. 337. According to the author, the term "whisperings" alludes to the secret denunciations.

216. Jules Isaac, *Jésus et Israël,* p. 93.

217. History reports five episodes concerning Pilate—three reported by Flavius Josephus, one by Luke, and the last by Philo of Alexandria. All unanimously describe Pilate as strongly anti-Jewish, cruel, and very unpopular among the Jews of both Palestine and the Diaspora. (Cf. Jules Isaac, *Jésus et Israël,* pp. 316-318.)

218. Cf. Daniel-Rops, *Jesus and His Times,* p. 517; and Isaac, *Jésus et Israël,* pp. 341-343.

219. Cf. James 5:1-6. The apostle accuses the rich of having condemned and killed the Righteous Man. The priestly caste, known for its affluence and its rapacity (see above) is seen here.

220. According to certain historians, Jules Isaac tells us, "the Sanhedrin had in religious affairs the broadest jurisdiction possible, the right to condemn to death as well as the right of execution. This is demonstrated by several capital executions carried out during the period from the time of the crucifixion of Jesus to the destruction of the Temple (e.g., the execution of Stephen, Acts 6:12 ff.; 7:58 ff.; of James, reported by Flavius Josephus, *Jewish Antiquities* 20.9.1; and of the daughter of a priest, T.B. Sanhedrin 7:2, 52b). Hence one can deduce that Jesus, having been crucified and not stoned, must have been judged and condemned by the Romans, not by the Jews." *Jésus et Israël,* p. 409. (Cf. also David Flusser, *Jésus,* pp. 129, 137, 138.)

221. According to Daniel-Rops, it was about 5:00 a.m. (cf. *op. cit.,* p. 422).

222. According to the majority of historians, it was not until the fourth century that the accusation of deicide arose. (Cf. Marcel Simon, *Verus Israel,* and F. Lovsky, *Antisémitisme et Mystère d'Israël.*)

223. See, for example, the translation of Isaiah 53:8 in the Bible of Zadok Kahn.

224. On this subject see G. Friedmann, "Antisémitisme et personnalité" *juive,* in *Fin du peuple juif,* pp. 317 ff.

225. See Luther's tract, *Dass Jesus Christus ein geborner Jude sei.*

226. E. Amado Lévi-Valensi, *La Racine et la Source,* p. 99.

227. Cited by Max Picard in *Le monde du silence,* p. 184.

228. *Jésus et Israël*, p. 558.

229. E. Amado Levi-Valensi, *op. cit.*, p. 21. (Cf. R. Loewenstein, *Psychanalyse de l'Antisémitisme.*)

230. A classic example of this is the use of the word *Baal*. This term means "husband" and was originally used in that sense until the day when it was assimilated to the Phoenician god of the same name. From that time the door was open to syncretism between the husband of Israel and the pagan god. The prophets thoroughly purified their language from the word Baal (cf. Hosea 11:18; A. Neher, *Langue hébraïque et civilisation biblique*, p. 11).

231. *Nostra Aetate* 4, 2b.

232. Cf. E. Amado Levi-Valensi, *op. cit.*, p. 24.

233. Cf. *Ibid.*, p. 24.

234. Cf. our article, "La vocation à la difference," in *Conscience et Liberté* No. 8 (International Revue of Religious Liberty).

235. *L'homme révolté*, p. 39.

236. *I and Thou*, p. 11.

237. Aboth 1:1.

238. *La Talmud et ses maîtres*, p. 25.

239. Article "Tradition."

240. Article "Tradition."

241. Cf. among so many others: Christian authors such as the Catholic C. Tresmontant, in *Essai sur la pensée hébraïque*, p. 95 and ff.; the Protestant Oscar Cullmann, in *Immortality of the Soul, or Resurrection of the Dead?*; and Jewish authors such as Josue Jehouda, in *Le monothéisme, doctrine de l'unité*, p. 32 ff.; Henri Baruk, in *Connaissance de l'homme au XXᵉ siècle*, p. 50 ff.; Robert Aron, *Lettre ouverte à l'Église de France*, p. 107 ff.

242. Vol. III, p. 498.

243. *Présence de l'Éternité*, p. 151.

244. See the article "Immortality of the Soul." Robert Aron explains the phenomenon thus: "I know as a historian that in the history of Israel the belief in conscious and individual survival after death was born in a precise moment of a moral crisis precipitated by the apparent injustice of fate, i. e., about the year 167 B.C., at the moment of the national uprising against the persecutions of Antiochus Epiphanes. Jews had perished in the service of their country and their God—an intolerable scandal, unacceptable to the hearts of the survivors, who sought and sought from the Supreme Being justifications, explanations, excuses. They found them in the belief in the immortality of the soul. *Is facit cui prodest* . . . , as a maxim of the legal profession puts it. That proves that survival after death is a necessity for the human heart, but it does not prove that it is true. . . . Let us be careful not to mistake our wishes, or our needs, for realities." *Op. cit.*, pp. 110, 111.

245. "La Bible et le Problème de l'au-celà," in *Revue de Théologie et l'Action évangélique*, p. 42.

246. *Op. cit.*, p. 83. On this subject see also the thesis of Jean Zurcher, *The Nature and Destiny of Man*, and that of R. Martin-Achard, *De la morte à la résurrection*. The first author approaches the question by putting it on a philosophical level. The second undertakes a study of the biblical conception and therefore addresses it on the exegetical, theological, and historical level.

The two methods reach the same conclusion: monistic anthropology such as found in the Bible cannot be compromised with the dualism implied in the idea of the immortality of the soul.

247. *Op. cit.*, p. 32. In this connection the psychiatrist H. Baruk notes that the movement of which Jéhouda avails himself is in harmony with the most recent scientific data about personality; it unites the wisdom of the past (the Bible) with that of the future (science). Among the scholars who have given up the dualistic view, we must mention among others Dr. Alexis Carrel (in *Man the Unknown*).

In fact, one can find in the Bible the modern conception of "psychosomatics." Man was considered as quite absolutely indivisible. Note how his physical life influenced his psychic life, and vice versa (cf. Proverbs 3:7, 8; 4:20-22). Hence the importance accorded in the Bible to dietary laws, to bodily hygiene and sanitation (cf. 1 Corinthians 3:16, 17; Leviticus 10:8-11; 11; etc.). The religion of biblical man had to embrace *all* the levels of his being (cf. 1 Thessalonians 5:23; 2 Corinthians 7:1). It is the whole man who is involved in his relationship with God (cf. Ecclesiastes 12:15 in the Hebrew text, *kol haadam* = the whole man).

248. Jerusalem Talmud, Shebith 4 (p. 365).

249. Jerusalem Talmud, Berakoth 2 (p. 37).

250. It was not until 1513, under the influence of the Lateran Council, that the dogma of natural immortality of the soul was finally proclaimed officially. The new bull, however, provoked more than one strong reaction—that of Luther being especially notable. The great Reformer relegated this dogma to the list of "the monstrous fables which comprise the Roman dunghill." (Cf. Petavel-Ollif, *Le problème de l'immortalité*, II, p. 77, and RHPR 198, p. 496 ff.).

251. *Dialogue with Trypho* 80.3-4.

252. That care which the rabbis and the fathers of the Church exercised in continually going back to the verses of Scripture in order to establish their arguments shows how much it represented for them the absolute criterion of the truth—the judge to which it was always necessary to resort.

253. On this question see in particular the work of T. Boman, *Hebrew Thought Compared with Greek*, and that of Cl. Tresmontant, *Essai sur la pensée hébraïque.*

It is well, however, to state the matter carefully. The contrast between the two modes of thought is not so absolute as these authors may lead us to understand. Nevertheless, the method of starkly contrasting them is a practical procedure for referring to them, in order to classify them at least schematically as profound and general tendencies of the cultures which they represent.

254. The apostle Peter expressed it well: "No prophecy ever came by the will of man, but men moved by the Holy Spirit spoke from God." 2 Peter 1:21.

On this subject, see the remarkably fine analysis by André Neher in his book, *The Prophetic Existence*, p. 317 ff., where the author reflects on, among other things, the burden of the prophetic calling.

255. It was at Anathoth, a small Levitical town north of Jerusalem, that Abiathar, stripped of his priestly functions, took refuge together with his family for a perpetual banishment. Thus was fulfilled the curse that had been pronounced on the house of Eli, of whom he was a descendant (cf. 1 Kings 2:26, 27; 1 Samuel 2:30-35).

256. In Ecclesiastes 12:15, Deuteronomy 5:29; 6:2; 8:1, etc., the fear of God is associated with the keeping of the commandments, and in Deuteronomy 10:20; 13:5, etc., the idea of fear is associated with that of love. S. Plath supplies a table of this usage in his book, *Furcht Gottes: Der Begriff Yra im Alten Testament*, Arbeiten zur Theologie, 2nd series, vol. 2, p. 33. Cf. also Reinhold Sander, *Furcht und Liebe im palästinensischen Judentum* (Beitrage zur Wissenschaft vom Alten und Neuen Testament, IV, 16, 16-68). Cf. Paul Jouon, *Crainte et peur en hébreu biblique*–Etude

de lexicographie et de stylistique. *Biblica,* vol. VI.

257. In his study on the theology of the Maharal of Prague, André Neher devoted a whole chapter to this matter of the fear of God. The profound and original reflections of the Jewish thinker warn us against all neat schematizations of this subject and provide essential perspectives for the comprehension of this biblical concept. Cf. *Le puits de l'Exil,* p. 213 ff.

258. It is in this sense that we must understand the biblical expression of "a jealous God." It belongs to the marriage imagery, which describes the relationship between God and His wife, Israel. The jealousy of God is a corollary of His love.

259. Cf. Psalms 139; 11:4, 5; 1 Chronicles 28:9; Hebrews 4:13; etc.

260. The verb is used only in reference to God.

261. Cf. Deuteronomy 28:10, where the two verbs are in parallelism. The Egyptian language also attests the same connection with reference to the verb NRJ. (Cf. Louis Derousseaux, *La crainte de Dieu dans l'Ancien Testament,* pp. 25, 26.)

262. *La culture trahie par les siens,* p. 36.

263. From Genesis to Malachi, "last canonical prophet of the Bible" (cf. A. Neher, *Essence du prophétisme).*

264. In Hebrew, as in Greek, it is the same word (*malakh, angelos).* Cf. Malachi 3:1, 23 in the Hebrew Bible (3:1; 4:5 in the Christian Bibles) and Revelation 14:6.

265. The word *remember* is itself a reference to something already known. It is true that the Israelites had to take the Sabbath into account even before the revealing of the Ten Commandments, as can be seen in connection with the giving of the manna (cf. Exodus 16:22-30). This requirement of God is very old; the Bible has it going back to the Creation (cf. Genesis 2:1-3).

266. Cf. above our chapter on "The Fear of God." One encounters this association between Fear of God and Creation in Psalm 33:9, a psalm which is still today a part of the Jewish liturgy for the Sabbath.

267. Placing the application of this commandment on the level of God, that is to say, beyond time, in order to interpret it "mystically" as not meaning a specific day, or "prophetically" as a long period, therefore constitutes a complete misunderstanding. It is the seventh day of the week *of man* which God blessed and set apart. "The Sabbath was made for man" and not for God. It has to do with a specifically human time.

Furthermore, the Hebrew text (of Genesis 2:1-3), though it is commonly invoked in support of the mystical or prophetic notions of the Sabbath, simply does not authorize such speculation. The verbs having God as their subject in this passage (He rested, blessed, and set apart the seventh day) are used in a manner characteristic of the historical genre (imperfect with waw-conversive).

When, for example, it was a matter of narrating the episodes in the life of a patriarch, or the more general history of Israel, the Hebrew writer indeed always resorted to this particular verbal mode. Understanding this verse of Genesis as if it were concerned with a time to come or a symbol would oblige one to read all the historical narratives in the Bible in the same sense.

In any case, the Creation text speaks explicitly of days of twenty-four hours with an evening and a morning. The expression which designates the first day already announces this fact to us sufficiently: *Yom ahad* =day one (with a cardinal number; the days which follow are qualified with ordinal numbers—second, third, etc.), an expression without ambiguity, which is used systematically throughout the Bible in the sense of a day of twenty-four hours.

The Sabbath which is in question does not refer to a long period or to a symbol; it is a concrete day which has an evening and a morning, a day intrinsic to human time—of twenty-four hours, a historical day.

268. Christ was resurrected on the first day of the week (cf. Matthew 28:1, 6); that is, on Sunday. Men have thus sought to justify the adoption of that day as the memorial of that event. But nothing in the teaching of Jesus and the apostles authorizes such a substitution. This line of argument did not appear until relatively late, in order to provide a rationale for a custom which had little by little infiltrated the Christian citadel under pagan influence.

For further reading material similar to Drinking at the Sources, *the following volumes are published by the same publisher.*

Patriarchs and Prophets—*a review of Old Testament times from Creation to the end of King David's life.*

Prophets and Kings—*an overview of Israel's history from Solomon's reign to Malachi.*

God Cares—*a remarkable study of the book of Daniel, written for the average young person as well as for the scholar.*

Order from the Pacific Press Publishing Association
Mountain View, CA 94042